WILLIAM ROSENAU

ACKNOWLEDGING LIMITS
Police Advisors and Counterinsurgency in
AFGHANISTAN

A joint publication of CNA and Marine Corps University Press

CNA Corporation

4825 Mark Center Drive

Alexandria, Virginia 22311

www.cna.org

Marine Corps University Press

3078 Upshur Avenue

Quantico, Virginia 22134

www.tecom.usmc.mil/mcu/mcupress

Acknowledging Limits: Police Advisors and Counterinsurgency in Afghanistan.

© 2011 by CNA Corporation. All rights reserved.

Second Printing 2012

PCN 10600004400

Published by Marine Corps University Press, Quantico, VA.

For sale by the Superintendent of Documents, U.S. Government Printing Office
Internet: bookstore.gpo.gov Phone: toll free (866) 512-1800; DC area (202) 512-1800
Fax: (202) 512-2104 Mail: Stop IDCC, Washington, DC 20402-0001

ISBN 978-0-16-089193-9

Contents

Acronyms
and Abbreviations

ABP	Afghan Border Police
ALP	Afghan Local Police
ANA	Afghan National Army
ANCOP	Afghan National Civil Order Police
ANP	Afghan National Police
BDD	Border District Development
CDI	Civilian Defense Initiative
CJTF-Phoenix	Combined Joint Task Force–Phoenix
CSTC-A	Combined Security Transition Command–Afghanistan
DOD	U.S. Department of Defense
EUPOL	European Union Police Mission
FDD	Focused District Development
FOB	Forward Operating Base
GAO	U.S. Government Accountability Office

IED	Improvised explosive device
ISAF	International Security Assistance Force
ISCI	Interim Security for Critical Infrastructure
MoI	Ministry of Interior
MP	Military Police
NATO/ISAF	North Atlantic Treaty Organization/ International Security Assistance Force
NTM-A	NATO Training Mission–Afghanistan
OPTEMPO	Operational tempo
PMT	Police Mentoring Team
PRT	Provincial Reconstruction Team
QRF	Quick-Reaction Force
RGR	Royal Gurkha Rifles
RTC	Regional Training Center
SWAT	Special Weapons and Tactics

Preface and
Acknowledgments

This monograph explores police mentoring in Afghanistan by U.S. and UK military forces during the 2007–2009 period. In a series of 10 vignettes, this study examines efforts to advise, train, and support elements of the Afghan National Police (ANP) in northern, eastern, and southern Afghanistan. These vignettes explore the mentoring of ANP units, as well as the advising of individual chiefs of police at the district and province levels.

This study would not have been possible without the generous assistance of American and British soldiers and Marines who gave many hours of their time in interviews and follow-on communications with the author. The author would also like to acknowledge Lieutenant Colonel Troy Wright, USMC, of the Joint Center for International Security Force Assistance, who facilitated key interviews, and the Irregular Warfare Community of Interest, whose members helped identify and locate interview subjects.

The author would also like to thank CNA's Connie Custer, Karin Duggan, Megan Katt, Jerry Meyerle, Rebecca Martin, Eric Thompson, and Lee Woodard. Finally, the author thanks the Marine Corps University Press, in particular Jim Caiella, Andrea Connell, Steve Evans, Robert Kocher, Shawn Vreeland, and Ken Williams.

Map of
Vignette Locations

Introduction

The role of the police is an important but largely overlooked aspect of contemporary counterinsurgency and stability operations. Although academic and policy specialists have examined the role of police in postconflict environments, the question of how police should be organized, trained, and equipped for counterinsurgency campaigns has received little systematic attention.[1] Similarly, U.S. military doctrine and the professional military literature, while not ignoring the subject entirely, do not consider it in any systematic way.[2] This gap is particularly ironic, given the prominent role that soldiers and Marines have played in training indigenous police and other security forces in counterinsurgency campaigns from Vietnam to Afghanistan.

If the broader topic of police and counterinsurgency is underexamined, the subject of mentoring—that is, advising, training, and partnering with—foreign police forces is even more neglected. American Marines, soldiers, and other military personnel preparing to deploy to Afghanistan for the police mentoring mission have few sources of information and analysis available to them. This monograph addresses that gap. Using a series of 10 vignettes, this report examines in depth the experiences of individual American and British soldiers and Marines who served as mentors in Afghanistan during the 2007–2009 period.

Approach

It should be noted that this study is not an assessment of the Afghan police. Nor is it an evaluation of the U.S. and North Atlantic Treaty Organization/International Security

---

[1] An important recent exception is David H. Bayley and Robert M. Perito, *The Police in War: Fighting Insurgency, Terrorism, and Violent Crime* (Boulder, CO: Lynne Rienner Publishers, 2010).

[2] James S. Corum, "Training Indigenous Forces in Counterinsurgency: A Tale of Two Insurgencies," U.S. Army Strategic Studies Institute, March 2006, www.strategicstudiesinstitute.army.mil/pubs/summary.cfm?q=648, accessed 15 June 2010. U.S. Army Field Manual 3-24, *Counterinsurgency*, widely considered the military's most important doctrinal statement on counterinsurgency, devotes fewer than seven pages to the subject of police and counterinsurgency. "Network analysis and other analytical tools," on the other hand, receives 28 pages.

Assistance Force (NATO/ISAF) assistance programs to the Afghan National Police (ANP). Instead, by focusing intensively on the experiences of individual mentors, this study provides a set of high-resolution pictures that illustrate the challenges, frustrations, and demands associated with mentoring the ANP. Although focused on mentoring the police in Afghanistan, this work is likely to be relevant to advisory missions in other austere and unstable environments—particularly those in which local internal security forces lack basic skills, equipment, organization, and legitimacy.

Drawing on long-form interviews supplemented with primary- and secondary-source materials, these vignettes explore how mentors worked to build the ANP at the district level.[3] A number of the vignettes also describe the mentoring of specialized units within the ANP, including the Afghan National Civil Order Police (ANCOP) and the Afghan Border Police (ABP).[4] In addition, several of them consider the mentoring of provincial and district chiefs of police.

However, these vignettes do not purport to present a complete picture. They focus on one period of time, albeit one in which mentoring activities had expanded considerably. Some provinces such as Helmand are more represented than others. As with any research project, time and resource constraints limited the number and variety of interview subjects.[5] Interviewing—or even locating—more than a relative handful of police mentors proved to be impossible. Written records were unavailable to confirm or enhance the information generated through interviews. Ideally, this study would have been rounded out by interviewing Afghan policemen, government officials, and ordinary citizens who came in contact with the police who had received U.S. or British mentoring.

Nevertheless, these snippets are of value for anyone seeking an understanding of ANP mentoring, despite the fact that they do not offer a complete picture of the people, cir-

---

[3] Unless otherwise indicated, all quotations in this study are taken from the author's interviews with U.S. and UK police mentors.

[4] In addition to ANCOP and the border police, the ANP is composed of the Afghan Uniformed Police, who make up the vast majority of the country's officers. The ANP also includes the Counternarcotics Police of Afghanistan and smaller, specialized forces responsible for counterterrorism, customs, and criminal investigations. Mentors typically used "ANP" as a generic term for all Afghan police.

[5] A more comprehensive study could have included interviews with mentors from other Coalition countries, particularly Canada and Germany, as well as police advisors employed by contractors such as DynCorp International.

cumstances, and events. In essence, these should be viewed as individual but struc-
tured perspectives. This focus on individuals offers advantages. In Afghanistan, counterinsurgency is waged village by village, district by district—and man by man. By looking
intensely at individual Marines and soldiers who mentored the ANP, it is possible to create a richly textured set of narratives that will resonate with the members of the armed
forces who are preparing to deploy to Afghanistan.[6]

Mentoring the Afghan National Police

As shown throughout the vignettes, soldiers and Marines were faced with police units
riddled with corruption, drug use, incompetence, and poor leadership. Recruits, drawn
from the lowest rungs of village life, were hobbled by illiteracy and, in some cases, physical and mental shortcomings. Senior police leaders routinely robbed their men of their
pay and equipment.

Preyed on by their superiors, policemen in turn preyed on the populations they were
meant to protect and serve. In many districts, the ANP's predatory behavior turned the
public against the police and cut off the flow of information from the population that is
essential for effective counterinsurgency. Police abuses also served as a major recruiting
tool for the Taliban.[7] Alienated from the public, poorly led and motivated, and often
thrust into combat conditions, the ANP were easy and ripe targets for the insurgents.

Such circumstances placed considerable demands on the American and British mentors. Looking back on their experiences, most could point to at least a few successes.
Accomplishments were typically small, and often short-lived: an apparent drop in police
corruption and drug use, for example, or evidence of growing pride and improved morale
within the ANP. Given the high motivation and problem-solving attitude prevalent
throughout the U.S. and UK officer and senior noncommissioned officer corps, it is perhaps not surprising that these individuals were eager to highlight perceived successes.

---

[6] For stylistic reasons, the vignettes are written in the past tense.

[7] Captured insurgents often "mention the police as the reason for joining in the first place,"
according to a senior British army commander. Richard Norton-Taylor, "Afghan Police Failings
Fuelling Taliban Recruitment," *Guardian* (London), 3 June 2010,
http://www.guardian.co.uk/world/2010/jun/03/afghanistan-police-fuel-taliban-recruitment,
accessed 16 June 2010. For more on police malfeasance as an insurgent recruiting theme, see
Antonio Giustozzi, *Koran, Kalashnikov and Laptop: The Neo-Taliban Insurgency in Afghanistan* (New
York: Columbia University Press, 2008), 62.

However, the subjects of these interviews were just as willing to identify shortfalls, deficiencies, and outright failures. As a number of mentors freely admitted, the seemingly modest goal of establishing what one British army officer called a "disciplined, professional force" proved to be elusive. Among other things, these vignettes illustrate the limits to what any individual mentor can expect to accomplish during his relatively short tour in Afghanistan.

Key Themes

Given the country's fractious nature, and the highly localized requirements of any successful campaign against insurgents, general observations concerning any aspects about counterinsurgency should be offered (and taken) with caution. That said, five important themes stand out in looking across the 10 vignettes.

Learning to Live with Police Corruption

By all accounts, nearly every institution associated with the Afghan state, including the Afghan National Army (ANA), was riddled with what in Western terms is considered corruption—that is, "the abuse of entrusted power for private gain."[8] As made clear in nearly every vignette, corruption among the Afghan police was effectively universal.

But there were degrees of corruption. Some illicit practices could be considered a survival mechanism. With salaries low even by Afghan standards, many policemen engaged in petty theft and pilfering (such as selling gasoline intended for police vehicles) to provide for their families. While hardly desirable, such behavior is understandable.

Less defensible was the widespread predatory behavior by the police. In some districts, policemen were victims of their own superior officers who stole their salaries or demanded a portion of their pay. Even more troubling was the ANP's abuse of the public. In many districts it preyed openly on the local population—stealing food from bazaars, robbing houses during police raids, and shaking down drivers and passengers along roadways. In Paktia Province, for example, a U.S. Army mentor noted that the police frequently ambushed the colorfully decorated multipurpose *jingha* (jingle) trucks along the Khost-Gardez Pass and stole their cargo. Such criminality was obviously inimical to

---

[8] The definition is from Transparency International, "Frequently Asked Questions About Corruption," www.transparency.org/news_room/faq/corruption_faq, accessed 22 June 2010.

good order and discipline. Moreover, it antagonized the very people the ANP were meant to protect.

Most mentors came to realize that creating a corruption-free force was simply unachievable. The challenge for police advisors was to determine what level of corruption was acceptable. In the judgment of most, petty pilfering of police supplies was tolerable, but stealing from the public, peddling drugs, and selling weapons to the Taliban represented "red lines."

As shown in several of the vignettes, mentors believed that measures such as holding the Afghan police to high standards, demonstrating to the Afghans the importance of professional conduct, and reducing the opportunities for police thievery (paying salaries through cell phones, for example) seemed to mitigate corruption.

But as a number of the vignettes also illustrated, apparent improvements were often short-lived, with the ANP quickly reverting to their old, corrupt ways. Moreover, as the Police Mentoring Team (PMT) commander in Now Zad discovered, corruption could reach levels that made it impossible for mentors to develop the trust and respect for the Afghan police necessary for effective mentoring.

Acknowledging Limits

Nearly all of the mentors detected at least some indications of progress among the Afghan police. An advisor in northern Afghanistan considered the ANCOP personnel he mentored to be professional and disciplined. In Garmsir District, a U.S. Marine mentor observed improved relations between the ANP and district residents. And in Nawa-I-Barakzayi District, the Marine PMT commander saw a growing esprit de corps and lower levels of corruption and drug abuse among the police.

But in many cases, progress appeared to be fleeting. As mentioned above, the police frequently slipped back into their old patterns. The nature of the environment in which they operated was part of the problem. In areas with particularly high levels of insurgent activity, such as southern and southeastern Afghanistan, policing was a high-risk profession, with ANP casualty rates far surpassing those of the ANA.

Given these perilous circumstances, it was hardly surprising that the police were reluctant to go out on patrol and perform operations that placed their lives at risk. Drugs were readily available to relieve boredom and alleviate despair. Opportunities to augment their salaries through crime and corruption were plentiful.

Mentors could make improvements at the margins, but there were clear limits to what they could reasonably expect to change during a 7- or 12-month tour. Some enduring problems, such as low police pay, dangerous working conditions, and a culture in which drug use was widely tolerated, were beyond the power of individual mentors to solve.

Perhaps the most formidable problem was the lack of human capital. The quality of police recruits was poor, which was a reflection of the village-level destitution, and the Afghan belief that the ANP was a reasonable career path for physically and mentally feeble young men.

For the mentors, frustration was a natural by-product of such circumstances. But as a British police advisor in Helmand concluded, it was important to overcome an understandable desire to accomplish as much as possible during a relatively short tour. A police mentor, he said, should focus "not on what I can do, but what I can do for the next guy."

Looking Beyond the Official Police

In Afghanistan, as in other counterinsurgency campaigns, the American approach has emphasized the importance of "winning" local populations over to the side of the government by building the legitimacy of the state. According to this line of reasoning, legitimacy increases as the state is increasingly able to deliver essential public goods, such as education, transportation, and security.

Establishing a uniformed, government police presence across Afghanistan is a pillar of this approach. But as a number of the mentors discovered, the goal of building the ANP was sometimes in conflict with the more immediate task of establishing local security. With the Afghan police unable to provide security, mentors looked beyond the ANP to unofficial security forces. Acting on their own initiative, these mentors adopted unorthodox approaches that could have been drawn from the U.S. Army Special Forces' unconventional warfare repertoire.

In Ghazni Province, a U.S. Army mentor, faced with chronic violence and lawlessness along the main highway, engaged an ethnic leader to restore order. In exchange for fuel from the Americans, Hazara militiamen manned checkpoints and succeeded in keeping both insurgents and ordinary bandits off the roadway.

In an area around the Khost-Gardez Pass, another U.S. Army mentor learned that a number of elders were eager to defend their villages from insurgents. He began providing them with AK-47 assault rifles and ammunition on a limited basis and with the understanding that any misuse of these weapons would result in swift retribution from U.S. forces. The effort came under criticism by some senior American officials, although ironically a similar initiative later became U.S. policy.

The rural areas of Afghanistan have a long history of providing for their own security and administration of justice. Throughout the countryside, law enforcement was usually the responsibility of local, traditional authorities rather than the Afghan government. Given the depredations of militias during the 1980s and 1990s, it is understandable that U.S. officials were reluctant to support unofficial armed groups. This concern was shared by a British police mentor in Helmand who feared that the U.S. special operations forces' attempts to build local self-defense forces could result in the creation of new and potentially destabilizing militias. Ultimately, he was able to persuade U.S. military commanders to integrate the village forces into the ANP and make them part of the country's formal justice structure.

Supporting informal security forces will not be appropriate in every circumstance in Afghanistan. Their legitimacy, capacity, and potential contribution must be considered on a case-by-case basis. At the very least, mentors should be alert to the possibility that security and justice can sometimes be provided by institutions that are outside the formal Afghan state. It is clear, however, that local, village-based security forces in Afghanistan—as in many other conflict zones—have become a significant part of counterinsurgency. Under the Afghan Local Police (ALP) program, NATO/ISAF expects to enlist tens of thousands of rural residents in community-based security forces—a development General David H. Petraeus has reportedly characterized as a counterinsurgency "game changer."[9] Members of the ALP, who receive uniforms, weapons, and a stipend from the Afghan MoI (Ministry of Interior), are intended to "compensate for shortfalls in the ANP,"[10] according to NATO/ISAF, and serve as a first line of defense against insurgents by "keep[ing an] eye out for bad guys—in their neighborhoods, in their communities," in the words of a Pentagon spokesman.[11]

Understanding Police Roles and Missions

The vignettes illustrate the fact that the ANP was often mentored to engage in activities that few Westerners would recognize as policing. In Qalat District, for example, the high levels of insurgent violence, combined with the very limited capabilities of the Afghan personnel, required the PMT to focus on developing the ANP's basic organizational, leadership, and tactical skills. To the PMT commander, it seemed apparent that what the district needed—and what was achievable, at least in the near term—was a paramilitary force rather than a Western-style crime-fighting agency.

Indeed, across southern and eastern Afghanistan, the ANP was employed as light infantry—equipped with machine guns and rocket-propelled grenades—and engaged in firefights with the Taliban. In such circumstances, the ANP were police in name only. As a former police chief in southern Afghanistan explained in 2007, his officers were ex-

---

[9] Kate Clark, "For a Handful of Dollars: Taleban Allowed to Join ALP," Afghan Analysts Network, http://aan-afghansistan.com/index.asp?id=1419, accessed 5 March 2011.

[10] NATO/ISAF, "Afghan National Security Forces," Media Backgrounder, www.isaf.nato.int/images/stories/File/factsheets/1667-10_ANSF_LR_en2.pdf, accessed 5 March 2011.

[11] Alissa J. Rubin, "Afghans to Form Local Forces to Fight Taliban," *New York Times*, 15 July 2010. The U.S. Marines have launched their own community-based security program in Marjah District, Helmand Province. Under the Interim Security for Critical Infrastructure (ISCI) program, the Marines have raised and financed a force of some 800 men designed to prevent the Taliban from reinfiltrating the district. For more on ISCI, see Saeed Shah, "New Militia Bring Security, and Worries, to Marjah, Afghanistan," McClatchy Newspapers, 2 March 2011, http://www.mcclatchydc.com/2011/03/01/109644/new-militia-brings-security-and.html#, accessed 10 March 2011; and "More Please, Sir," *Economist* (London), 24 February 2011, www.economist.com/node/18233390, accessed 10 March 2011.

pected to perform like "little soldiers . . . .We do extra work that is not police work. Firing rockets is not the job of police."[12]

Some mentors saw police roles and missions differently. As a military policeman in the U.S. Marines, the PMT commander in Garmsir brought a law enforcement perspective to mentoring. While accepting that the ANP needed skills for surviving violent encounters with the Taliban, the PMT leader believed that the Garmsir police should serve and protect the population—in other words, they should conduct what scholars have termed "core policing."[13]

The question of police roles and missions should be considered carefully by every mentor serving in Afghanistan. For the PMT commander in Qalat, focusing on the development of ANP "survival" skills made sense, given the extent of insurgent activity and the extensive level of security and justice services provided by informal, customary, and tribal institutions. In other areas of the country, however, such structures were less robust—or were suborned, infiltrated, or replaced by the Taliban. In such circumstances, a heavy emphasis on paramilitary training and operations led to a policing vacuum or, more ominously, the conceding of security and justice to the Taliban.

Among other things, mentors should consider the potential consequences of emphasizing one form of policing—paramilitary or "core"—over the other. In some circumstances, it may be possible to bridge this divide by pressing the ANA and the ANP to function together in contested or unstable districts, with the army providing the security "shell" necessary for the police to carry out more conventional law enforcement responsibilities.

The contradictions between paramilitary and core policing—or, to put it another way, between the police as a force versus the police as a service—is likely to become more

---

[12] Quoted in International Crisis Group, "Reforming Afghanistan's Police," Asia Report No. 138, 30 August 2007, 15.

[13] Bayley and Perito, *The Police in War*, 73–74. By deterring disorder, controlling violence, and providing "instant response," the police, according to Bayley and Perito, can win "hearts and minds" and in so doing enhance the legitimacy of the state, a key objective of contemporary Western counterinsurgency doctrine. A variation on this concept is "democratic policing," that is, "policing that uses minimal force, is relatively incorrupt, and provides reasonably impartial assistance and redress within an accountable and known Western-style criminal justice framework." Alice Hills, *Policing Post-Conflict Cities* (London: Zed Books, 2009), 66.

apparent as NATO/ISAF expands the ALP across the country. Although technically under the control of the MoI and ANP chain of command, the ALP has no powers of arrest. Moreover, the ALP is being trained by U.S. special forces personnel.[14] Taken together, this suggests that the ALP is likely to have a paramilitary rather than core policing orientation.

Mentoring's Human Dimension

For individuals preparing to deploy to Afghanistan, the final theme is perhaps of the greatest relevance and importance. The following vignettes illustrate the central role that personal relationships played in effective police mentoring. To be successful, advisors had to do more than impart technical skills—empathy (if not sympathy) and sensitivity were also essential. In the words of a British police advisor in Helmand, "It was about personal relationships, mutual respect, and not being arrogant. It was really about good manners."

Building such relationships began with showing an interest in the life stories and family histories of Afghan policemen. According to the U.S. Army mentor in Mazar-e Sharif, three or four long visits with a counterpart were the minimum required to begin building a relationship. Only after a relationship was established would the Afghans be willing to accept and act on the advice their mentors provided.

This personal interest, according to several advisors, helped mentors gain influence among the police. It also fostered self-confidence among the Afghan police—men who were typically from impoverished rural backgrounds and often burdened with physical and mental shortcomings.

Teaching by personal example was an important part of mentoring, particularly for U.S. Marines. Maintaining strict professionalism, respect, and discipline among advisory team members helped improve the outlook and performance of the ANP, according to the PMT commander in Nawa-I-Barakzayi District. For this advisor, successful mentoring meant instilling in the Afghans what was in essence a moral commitment to

---

[14] Brian Wagner, "ALP program starting in Shah Joy ," U.S. Air Forces Central, www.afcent.af.mil/news/story_print.asp?id=123240227, accessed 6 March 2011.

policing—that is, the belief that protecting and serving the public was an honorable profession.

Mentoring also required firmness. While showing that they cared about ANP officers on a personal level, the PMT also expected the police to live up to the standards that were set for them. In the words of the Nawa PMT leader, "We wouldn't accept excuses like 'my foot hurts.' At first we were worried about offending them, but then we learned that if you're soft, they won't respond."

Finally, mentors stressed the importance of allowing the Afghans to fail. Aware that there would come a time when the ANP would have to stand on its own—and without the "stiffening" effect of having the mentors present—mentors encouraged the police to make their own decisions, even if those choices were clearly wrong in the eyes of the advisors.

These themes—and the vignettes that follow—are not intended to be prescriptive. None will be relevant in all of Afghanistan's districts and provinces. Marines and other personnel deploying to Afghanistan should view them simply as a means for gaining insights into, and preparing for, the demands associated with training and advising the Afghan police.

Vignette 1

Police Mentoring Team
Qalat District, 2008

Police mentoring team (PMT) Swampfox arrived in Zabul Province in southwestern Afghanistan in April 2008.[15] Commanded by a major in the New York State National Guard, the team would spend the next six months mentoring the Afghan National Police (ANP) at stations and checkpoints in Qalat District, seat of the provincial capital.

Mentoring in Qalat

Swampfox was assigned to Qalat District, the seat of the provincial capital. Like many other PMTs in Afghanistan, the team was somewhat understrength, with 12 officers and noncommissioned officers instead of the 16 that were authorized. Also, like most PMTs operating in a less-than-permissive environment, most of Swampfox's personnel were part of the team's security force, although the PMT's commander repeatedly stressed that everyone was expected to perform a mentoring role as well.

The commander of PMT Swampfox had originally expected to mentor an Afghan National Army (ANA) unit, and his predeployment course for mentors at Fort Riley, Kansas, stressed combat skills, including advanced weapons training. "We spent more time on the machine-gun range than on cultural skills," he recalled.[16] He received a smattering of language training in Dari, the most widely spoken language in western and central Afghanistan. Shortly before the end of the course, he learned that he would be deploying to Zabul and began what he termed a "crash course" in Pashto, the principal language of the country's southwestern and southeastern provinces.

Although some of the PMT members had served previously in Afghanistan, none had experience as mentors. However, the team brought with it a set of skills that proved relevant in the context of police mentoring in Afghanistan. Swampfox was made up of reservists, who in civilian life worked as corrections officers, state policemen, lawyers, and other law-enforcement professionals.

---

[15] This vignette draws on the author's interviews, New York, 20 December 2009, and 23 February 2010, and subsequent e-mail communications.

[16] Bayley and Perito, *The Police in War*.

More broadly, the commander believed that his civilian position as a businessman gave him a degree of patience that was particularly useful in dealing with the Afghan police. "Everything's a negotiation with the Afghans," he recalled, "and I think my skills as a businessman in civilian life made me a better advisor."

Members of PMT Swampfox lived on a forward operating base in Qalat City that was located next door to one of the two police stations for which the team was responsible. The police also manned a checkpoint outside the city. In total, the mentors were responsible for about 115 to 200 police officers.

Chronically short of vehicles and fuel, the ANP used checkpoints as a means to monitor and control traffic flow along major roads. In theory, checkpoints, as population-control instruments, contributed to law enforcement and counterinsurgency. In practice, checkpoints were more often sources of income for the ANP, who used them to extract goods and revenue from vehicles and their passengers. Such predation helped reinforce the public's perception of the police as a corrupt and sinister force—a perception obviously inimical to the population-centric counterinsurgency strategy advanced by U.S. and Coalition leaders.

Police Mentoring Team Swampfox was responsible for about 115 to 200 police officers in the Qalat District.
(Photo courtesy of PMT Swampfox)

The Swampfox team mentoring included classroom training, but the police lacked patience to sit through such formal instruction. (Photo courtesy of PMT Swampfox)

Moreover, isolated and poorly defended checkpoints were highly vulnerable to insurgent attacks, and, given the ANP's lack of mobility, it was almost certain that reinforcements would be slow to arrive.

As the team discovered upon its arrival in Qalat, the district had no chief of police. An ANP colonel, who was the province's deputy police chief, served as the district's de facto chief. According to the PMT leader, the ANP colonel displayed remarkable professionalism and leadership by Afghan police standards:

> He showed up in a shirt and a tie, and the men were terrified of him. Lots of Afghans said the colonel was crooked, but he could accomplish things no one else could. He had been trained by the Soviets in Siberia, and he had been in the province for 30 years.

The men under the ANP colonel's command had recently been through the first cycle of Focused District Development, a police training program launched across Afghanistan in November 2007 by the Combined Security Transition Command–Afghanistan. In essence, the program sought to improve the effectiveness of the uniformed ANP by removing a district's entire police force and sending it for training at a provincial or regional facility. During the ANP's absence from the district, a unit of the Afghan National Civil Order Police, a relatively highly trained and disciplined national force, provided security and, ideally, demonstrated to the local population how a professional police force performed its duties.[17] After the local police returned to their district, PMTs would provide follow-on mentoring.

To reinforce the lessons learned at the training facility, this mentoring included classroom training. But like the personnel of many other PMTs, Swampfox members found that the Afghan police lacked the patience to sit through formal classes. The ANP was far more amenable to practical instruction, exercises, and patrolling under the watchful eyes of their mentors. Although some patrols were carried out in the bazaar and elsewhere in Qalat City, the PMT and the police spent far more time in the district's out-

---

[17] For more on FDD, see Robert M. Perito, "Afghanistan's Police: The Weak Link in Security Sector Reform," United States Institute of Peace, Special Report 227, August 2009, 5–6.

The National Guardsmen found that the police were better taught through practical exercises and instruction, and patrolling under the mentors' guidance. (Photo courtesy of PMT Swampfox)

lying villages. Patrolling with the ANP generated some positive results, in the team leader's judgment. "The police got confidence by our going out with them, even if it was only 2 of us and 13 of them," he said.

Through this mentoring, PMT Swampfox sought to reinforce basic military skills and discipline within the ANP. Given the level of insurgent violence in Qalat Province, "It was all about helping the police stay alive at that point," recalled the PMT commander.[18] Moreover, given the fact that the administration of justice in Qalat, as in much of the country, was provided by village *jirga*s (decision-making assemblies), the role of the police and other formal agencies was necessarily minor.[19] Jirgas, which typically comprised tribal elders, religious leaders, and other local notables, adjudicated civil disputes and minor offenses. Only when the most serious violent crimes had taken place—or in instances where the jirga's judgment was not accepted by the relevant parties—were the police called in. Western concepts of policing, in the PMT leader's view, were irrelevant in such circumstances. What was needed, he believed, was a paramilitary rather than a police force.

Fostering Popular Support

Although training the ANP in community policing and other Western forms of law enforcement was ruled out, the PMT did not neglect the central issue of improving police interaction with the local population. Effective counterinsurgency required the population to provide information to the security forces. But first, the ANP had to be trained to interact properly with local residents. Improving the ANP's relationship with the public was the thread running throughout much of the PMT's mentoring.

---

[18] In 2009, Afghan policemen were killed in the line of duty at roughly twice the rate of Afghan soldiers. Sean D. Naylor, "Forces in Discord: Distrust Between Afghan Army and Police Hampers U.S. Efforts," *Armed Forces Journal International*, July 2009, www.afji.com/2009/07/4231017, accessed 20 December 2010. For more on police casualties, see "Highlights: Afghan Police Issues 16–31 Dec 09: Interior Minister Outlines Police Priorities," Open Source Center, 13 January 2010.

[19] For more information on informal justice and security in Afghanistan, see Susanne Schmeidl and Masood Karokhail, "The Role of Non-State Actors in 'Community Based Policing': An Exploration of the Arbakai (Tribal Police) in South Eastern Afghanistan," *Contemporary Security Policy*, Vol. 30, No. 2 (August 2009); and The Liaison Office, "Linkages Between State and Non-State Justice Systems in Eastern Afghanistan: Evidence from Jalalabad, Nangarhar and Ahmad Aba, Paktia," May 2009, http://www.tlo-afghanistan.org/publications/working-paper-series/linkages-between-state-and-non-state-justice-systems-eastern-afgha, accessed 21 August 2010.

Swampfox personnel instructed the ANP on how to enter a village, treat the population and its property with respect, and engage with the appropriate elders. They also addressed the nagging problem of police checkpoints, a source of popular grievance with the ANP. The PMT that Swampfox replaced had recommended reducing the number of checkpoints in the district, and the commander enthusiastically agreed that what he termed the "toll booths and targets" should be consolidated. "I wanted to turn my checkpoint into a provincial training center for the ANP," the PMT commander said. "I tried to set up a firing range and do other things, but it was simply too hard to find qualified ANP instructors."

The commander also eliminated cordon and search operations, which he believed were "a complete waste of time." These intrusive searches failed to locate weapons or suspected insurgents, and, more important, they further alienated local residents.

To improve public perceptions of the ANP, the mentors initiated their own information operations. A supply of hand-cranked radios delivered to villages and access to local FM radio facilitated by U.S. Army Special Forces allowed the PMT to reach significant segments of the population. The team found an imam (leader of a mosque) willing to speak out against the Taliban, and the police colonel recorded messages for local radio. As the PMT commander recalled, the ANP colonel "told the audience: 'Any of my men do anything wrong, I want you to call me. Here's my number.'" Swampfox devised other psychological operations as well. Adopting one of the Taliban's signature techniques, the team helped the police create "night letters" to warn insurgents living in villages that the ANP was aware of their presence.

Finally, the mentors attempted to foster a public image of ANP competence and professionalism. The belief in "winning hearts and minds" has become something of a counterinsurgency cliché in recent years. Nonetheless, it is true that building a civilian population's belief that security forces have at least a chance of prevailing can be a powerful tool against insurgents.

Keeping the U.S. presence to a minimum and giving the Afghans credit for any successful police-related activities was crucial, in the PMT commander's judgment. "We always tried to stay in the background," he said. "You have to dedicate yourself to working in the background. I wouldn't join in meetings with elders. I would only sit down if they asked me specifically." Also, humanitarian assistance was delivered by ANP trucks rather than U.S. vehicles. Moreover, the team leader made certain that the police got credit in the local media. As he recalled, "There was no mention of the U.S., even though we killed a lot of bad guys after a night ambush that killed a Taliban commander."

Conclusion

PMT Swampfox's mission in Qalat ended in October 2008. In the view of its commander, the team, which trained approximately 250 policemen during its six months in the district, had improved the ANP's capabilities. For example, the ANP was able to carry out a number of targeted night raids against suspected Taliban compounds. "We'd get the guy before anyone was up," he explained. Such raids suggested not only a measure of ANP competence, but also an increased flow of information from the local population to the police—among other things, an indicator of greater public willingness to interact with the ANP.

Ultimately, however, the team's experiences highlight the clear limits to what a PMT could reasonably expect to achieve. The team demonstrated initiative and creative approaches to the profound challenges of mentoring the ANP. In helping the police learn how to survive in a dangerous environment and, more important, by working to improve the ANP's relationship with the local population, the PMT's mentoring reflected an understanding of what was required of the police in counterinsurgency. Yet the ANP in Qalat District remained hobbled by corruption, lack of leadership, and incompetence. Grave police shortcomings were hardly confined to Qalat, however—as of mid-2008, no ANP unit anywhere in Afghanistan was rated as "fully capable."[20]

---

[20] U.S. Government Accountability Office (GAO), *Afghanistan Security: U.S. Efforts to Develop Capable Afghan Police Forces Face Challenges and Need Coordinated, Detailed Plan to Help Ensure Accountability*, GAO-08-883T (Washington, DC: GAO, 18 June 2008), 6.

Police Training Mission
Khost-Gardez Pass, 2007–2008

During 2007 and 2008, a U.S. Army captain led a team of mentors in southeastern Afghanistan along the Khost-Gardez Pass, a key entryway through the Hindu Kush mountains.[21] The team had two missions. The first was to interdict the Taliban and secure the pass; the second was to partner with the Afghan National Army (ANA) and Afghan National Police (ANP)—"train with them, work with them, and build their capacity," according to the team leader.

Mentoring the Afghan National Army

The Khost-Gardez Pass is the central link between Khost Province and the city of Gardez, Paktia's provincial capital, and it functions as a main artery from the region into north-central Afghanistan. As the team discovered, the Taliban were not the only violent actors operating in and around the pass, but the identity of the fighters was not always clear. "We didn't know a lot about 'red' [adversary forces]," the team's commander recalled. "We knew they were not just Taliban. There were members of the Haqqani network.[22] And there were foreign fighters—it was difficult to tell their nationality, although our terps [interpreters] could tell they were outsiders."

U.S. infantry, cavalry, and artillery platoons partnered with the ANA, while a military police (MP) squad partnered with the ANP. The ANA quickly earned the respect of the mentoring team's commander. "We trusted and respected the ANA," he recalled. Living on

---

[21] Quotations in this vignette, unless otherwise noted, are from the author's interview, Alexandria, VA, 20 November 2009, and subsequent e-mail communications.

[22] Affiliated with the Taliban, the Haqqani network, whose origins can be traced to the anti-Soviet Afghan resistance movement, has been described as America's most lethal adversary in Afghanistan. For more on the network, see Commander NATO International Security Assistance Force, Afghanistan, and U.S. Forces, Afghanistan, "Commander's Initial Assessment," 30 August 2009, 2–6, www.media.washingtonpost.com/wp-srv/politics/documents/Assessment_Redacted_092109.pdf, accessed 25 November 2009; and Anand Gopal, "The Most Deadly U.S. Foe in Afghanistan," *Christian Science Monitor*, 1 June 2009, www.csmonitor.com/World/Asia-SouthCentral/2009/0601/p10s01-wosc.html, accessed 8 March 2010.

the forward operating base (FOB) with the Americans, and receiving the bulk of United States' attention and resources, the ANA was carefully nurtured. Afghan soldiers, he said, were highly motivated and eager to operate with their American counterparts. Afghan soldiers would wake up the commander in the middle of the night, or seek him out on the FOB, and propose their own ideas about missions. By the time the mentors left in 2008, the ANA was capable of carrying out successful operations on its own.

Glaring Police Shortfalls

The Afghan police were another matter. Unlike the ANA, they showed little initiative. Corruption within the force was endemic. The local population feared and hated the ANP, which routinely extracted "taxes" from travelers along the highway. "Jingle" (or *jingha*) trucks, the colorfully decorated multipurpose vehicles found across Central Asia, were favored targets for ANP predation. The police frequently ambushed the trucks at night and stole their cargo. One local police chief was notorious for hijacking the vehicles, according to the mentoring team commander. "In one instance, after the police chief claimed that the Haqqani network had burned a jingle truck, we found it parked behind the police station," he said. "There were times when I wanted to arrest the ANP."

The so-called "jingle" trucks moving through the Khost-Gardez Pass were frequent targets of the Afghan National Police. (U.S. Air Force photo)

The relatively strong performance of the ANA, and the continued shortcomings of the ANP, led the team leader to shift his focus from the army to the police halfway through his tour. The police faced a chronic shortage of supplies and equipment, and remained undertrained. "They had no budget, and after marksmanship training they'd be out of ammo," he recalled. Fuel was always in short supply, partly because the police had to drive to Kabul to refuel.[23] The team commander supplied them with fuel, but they typi-

---

[23] The distances involved are considerable. It is roughly 225 kilometers (140 miles) from Khost to Kabul.

cally sold it in the bazaar. "I didn't like it," he said, "but I understood that they had survival needs."

ANP morale was equally poor. One district police chief, nicknamed "Abe Lincoln," was aggressive, but proved to be atypical. "Occasionally we'd have the individual Afghan policeman who cared about the security of his district," the team chief recalled, "but unless he could muster sufficient cooperation by his comrades—and they never could—effective policing didn't happen." Also, the team chief remembered that "you never saw the same police twice" because of frequent desertions. "Many times," he recollected, "the police were simply afraid to leave their stations. They knew that if they did a good policing job, they would get a night letter [from the insurgents] threatening to cut their heads off." Moreover, the terrain was very isolating, which meant that police under attack would have a long time to wait for reinforcements.

Building the Afghan National Police

Rampant desertion and high casualties among the ANP meant that recruitment was an urgent priority, and the mentoring team leader met frequently with *shuras* (Islamic councils) to help fill police ranks. But poor pay, danger, and the level of contempt with which most villagers regarded the police were powerful disincentives to joining the force. One district subgovernor, rather than use his budget to fund his district's ANP, would instead hire villagers to be his personal bodyguards and drivers. These informal forces would drive ANP vehicles and carry weapons, and when stopped by Coalition forces would present permits from the subgovernor. Inducements and bargaining were therefore essential components of the team leader's interactions with the shuras. As he recalled, "We'd say: 'You owe the district subgovernor five people for the security forces. Give him five names of males to receive training and we'll dig a well.'" But more often than not, the elders would return to the village and come back with just two men who had never fired weapons before.

It was obvious to the mentors that building the most basic skills and creating a reasonably disciplined armed force was the critical first step. Toward that end, instruction focused on patrolling and other fundamental tactical skills, weapons handling and safety, and equipment maintenance. To alleviate ammunition shortages, policemen were brought into the FOB for marksmanship training. First-aid instruction provided by the Americans was intended to build confidence. Acquiring more advanced, police-specific skills, such as fingerprinting and criminal investigation, was well beyond the ANP's capabilities. In some cases, just getting the police to wear their uniforms was a challenge.

Rather, the stress was on building capabilities that the team leader believed would have an immediate impact on the insurgents and build the ANP's confidence and ability to survive in what were very dangerous circumstances. "We trained the police to get out in villages, talk to the locals, and gather intelligence," he said. However, the ANP, unlike the ANA, never reached the point where it could patrol on its own and would venture off the main road only when accompanied by Coalition forces.

The training provided to the ANP had an important psychological dimension. "I wanted to understand the human terrain," the team's commander said. "I found out where the police were from, where their loyalties were. Once you spent a lot of time with them, built personal relationships, and got to know them, you could get them to perform." Training, he related, made the ANP more confident and aggressive, but "they atrophied quickly. They made lots of excuses and didn't show up at their stations."

Village Self-Defense

The commander's continuing frustration with the ANP led him to consider new approaches to ensuring local security. Elders had been extremely reluctant to provide manpower for the ANA and ANP, but they often volunteered to secure their villages. The team's second-in-command, convinced that villagers were ready to defend themselves, suggested providing weapons on a selective basis. During late 2007, the mentors began providing a group of village elders with captured AK-47 rifles and ammunition. "The idea was to create a homegrown force with allegiance to the village," the team chief explained. He realized that it was impossible to guarantee the loyalty of every Afghan involved and that weapons might be used against Coalition or Afghan security forces. Therefore, he decided to hold the elders accountable:

ANP recruits stand in formation near Gardez in March 2007. (U.S. Air Force photo)

> We would let them select the people who received weapons. We would record the serial numbers and made it clear that if any weapons ended up in insurgent hands, or if my men took any fire from them, they'd suffer serious consequences. We told them we'd be back to check on them. This threat was meant to keep them honest.

These villages were not meant to operate in isolation. The mentors expected them to work through district subgovernors and to share information with the ANA, the ANP, and U.S. forces. Indeed, they were intended to generate "actionable" intelligence for counterinsurgency at the village level. "As we told the elders, 'You tell us where the bad guys are, and we'll help you protect your village,'" the team's commander recalled.

As far as some Americans were concerned, the mentors were engaged in militia building—a highly sensitive subject in Afghanistan. "This was a very touchy subject at the time," the team leader remembered, "and the idea was not well received." Although he came under sharp criticism, he left Afghanistan convinced that the village self-defense initiative held great promise.

By 2009, opinion had shifted, at least among the senior U.S. military leadership, who came to embrace the notion of supporting "homegrown" militias as a counterinsurgency tool. Under the Community Defense Initiative (CDI), the United States is reportedly spending $1.3 billion to assist indigenous self-defense forces in 14 parts of Afghanistan.[24] Echoing the approach made by mentors in 2007 and 2008, an unnamed senior U.S. military officer said that the goal of CDI "is to get people to take responsibility for their own security. In many places they are already doing that."[25]

Conclusion

The mentors operating along the Khost-Gardez Pass experienced many of the same frustrations that other police mentors have encountered across Afghanistan. Clearly neglected relative to the ANA, the Afghan police required moral and psychological as well as material support. Recognizing the ANP's profound shortcomings, mentors focused on the human dimension of mentoring—namely, the importance of establishing personal relationships with the ANP, and, through those ties, fostering a sense of confidence, self-worth, and aggression among the police.

Yet none of these efforts appeared to make any real impact on the ANP, whose performance, integrity, and professionalism continued to remain far below those of the ANA. The ANP was not necessarily a lost cause, but it was evident that prospects for es-

---

[24] Jon Boone, "U.S. Pours Millions into Anti-Taliban Militias in Afghanistan," *Guardian* (London), 22 November 2009, www.guardian.co.uk/world/2009/nov/22/us-anti-taliban-militias-afghanistan, accessed 9 March 2010.

[25] Dexter Filkins, "Afghan Militias Battle Taliban With Aid of U.S.," *New York Times*, 21 November 2009, www.nytimes.com/2009/11/22/world/asia/22militias.html, accessed 10 March 2010. The Afghan Local Police is the latest in a series of initiatives since 2008 to build local security forces to augment the Afghan security forces. For more on local security initiatives, see Mathieu Lefèvre, "Local Defense in Afghanistan: A Review of Government-Backed Initiatives," Afghanistan Analysts Network, AAN Thematic Report 03/2010, www.humansecuritygateway.com/documents/AAN_LocalDefenceAfghanistan.pdf, accessed 10 May 2010; Jon Boone, "U.S. Keeps Secret Anti-Taliban Militia on a Bright Leash," *Guardian* (London), 8 March 2010, www.guardian.co.uk/ world/2010/mar/08/us-afghanistan-local-defence-militia, accessed 12 March 2010; and Jason Motlagh, "Afghan Militias: The Perils of Trying to Duplicate Iraq," *Time* (online edition), 27 October 2010, www.time.com/time/world/article/0,8599,2027695,00.html, accessed 10 November 2010.

tablishing an even modestly capable force were dim. Faced with an urgent requirement to establish security along the Khost-Gardez Pass, the mentoring team commander sought alternatives to the police.

Certain that villagers were willing to defend themselves, he decided to provide captured enemy weapons to selected village elders. His initiative was unorthodox. Indeed, it could have been drawn from the U.S. Army Special Forces' unconventional warfare repertoire. Establishing indigenous, village-based security had long been recognized as an important counterinsurgency tool. Yet in 2007, anything that smacked of "militia-building" in Afghanistan was frowned upon by some Americans, and his initiative had an unfavorable reception. Today, building local self-defense forces remains controversial; however, it now has powerful advocates in the upper reaches of the U.S. military command who are eager to generate additional Afghan forces as quickly as possible.

A U.S. soldier supervises a checkpoint run by a local defense force in Kandahar Province in April 2010. (U.S. Army photo)

British Police Mentors
Helmand Province, 2008–2009

Since October 2007, the British counterinsurgency campaign in Helmand Province had emphasized a "population-centric" approach that mixed kinetic and nonkinetic means as required.[26] Security-sector reform—which included support to the Afghan National Police (ANP)—was an important priority in British policy.

During 2008–2009, a group of British police mentors advised the Afghan police in and around the provincial capital, Lashkar Gah. Five teams, each composed of 16 men, advised and trained the police. These teams included military policemen (MPs) and elements of the 2d Battalion, the Royal Gurkha Rifles (2d RGR).

No More "Drive-By" Mentoring

The immediate concern of the mentors was to improve the ANP's performance in Lashkar Gah. "If the local population perceived that the provincial governor was unable to secure his own capital, what hope was there in getting them to accept the government more broadly?" one British officer recalled. "We had to demonstrate success there."

Faced with stiff armed opposition from the Taliban in and around the city, police mentors spent most of their time simply holding ground. "But when a battle group got put in, this freed up the police mentors," recollected a British mentor.[27] With more troops on the ground providing security, the British teams could extend their area of operations to include districts outside the provincial capital.

---

[26] Unless noted otherwise, quotations in this vignette are from the author's interviews, Ministry of Defence, London, 3 February 2010, and subsequent e-mail communications. For more on British counterinsurgency strategy in Afghanistan, see Theo Farrell and Stuart Gordon, "COIN Machine: The British Military in Afghanistan," *Orbis*, Fall 2009, 665–83.

[27] A *battle group* is the British army term for a battalion-sized formation that brings together armor, infantry, artillery, and other assets into a combined arms team.

British troops patrol with the Afghan police in Musa Qala, Helmand Province.
(Photo courtesy of Andre Prudent)

The increased troop presence also freed up the British advisors to mentor the Afghans more intensively. "We needed to build our credibility with the ANP, so we decided no more 'drive-by' mentoring," according to one officer. Instead of living on their own bases, the British teams embedded with the Afghan police and lived with them 24 hours a day.

Living Off Their Wits

As the British discovered, the ANP had a will-o'-the-wisp quality. The police kept few records—perhaps not surprising in a province with a literacy rate of 4 percent—and it was unclear how many police there actually were.[28] Moreover, there was what one British officer termed a "shed full" of "known and unknown" police checkpoints. "We would go out and visit checkpoints, get names of policemen, [inventory] equipment, come back to headquarters, and put it in a database," he recalled.

---

[28] United Nations Development Program, *Afghanistan Human Development Report 2007*, cited in Naval Postgraduate School, Program for Culture & Conflict Studies, Helmand Provincial Overview, www.nps.edu/programs/ccs/Helmand.html, accessed 27 February 2010.

High levels of casualties and desertion added to the chaos surrounding police man- ning. "Two hundred police were recruited and trained [in one district], and they promptly ran away," recalled one British advisor. The police were highly vulnerable to bribes, and while the mentors did not approve of such corruption, the British understood it. Given their pitiful pay, the advisor said, "They had to sustain themselves by living off their wits." In an effort to reduce corruption, which included payroll-skimming by police offi- cials, he continued, "We started taking responsibility for pay, supervising it every step of the way."

Given attrition levels, recruiting fresh bodies to fill ANP ranks was critical, but the men- tors were underwhelmed by the Afghan recruitment pool. "In an Afghan family, the strong sons help on the farm, and the bright ones might get an education," said one British of- ficer, "but the one with a club foot, or a dodgy eye, he'd be told to go stand at a police checkpoint." The officer recalled village recruiting drives where elders would offer up men with one leg as potential policemen. "They thought that standing at a checkpoint was a good occupation for a guy with one leg—at least he wouldn't be a burden to his family," he said.

Rampant criminality and drug trafficking in the province made a difficult operating en- vironment even more violent and chaotic. "There was a big poppy season," one advisor recalled. "Ninety percent of the UK's heroin came from the province. A former provin- cial governor was involved in drugs, and he was trying to reassert his authority when we pitched up."

On visits to some villages, mentors discovered that elders clearly did not want to see the police. "They didn't want us," one mentor recalled. "They were complicit with the Taliban and the drug militias." But in other places the mentors encountered local strongmen with different attitudes toward the ANP. "In some places, the chief of police couldn't get anything done," the mentor said. "The local headman viewed the police as his personal force, and he would use them to guard his poppy fields."

Royal Gurkha Rifles

The British mentors attempted to train the ANP in a formal classroom setting, but the effort was fruitless. In the view of one advisor, the largely illiterate and undisciplined Afghan police were simply incapable of absorbing such forms of instruction. The police "were very immature and couldn't sit still, and were like children, really," he recalled. He therefore stressed practical demonstrations—showing how to man and operate a vehicle checkpoint, for example—which seemed to be more readily absorbed by the ANP. During encounters with the Taliban, he recalled, a number of Afghan policemen proved themselves to be "brave and enthusiastic" fighters.

ANP officers in the Musa Qala District.
(Photo courtesy of Andre Prudent)

The Gurkhas within the police mentoring teams displayed an ingrained talent for working with the Afghans. Recruited in Nepal and renowned for their professionalism, prowess, and tenacity, Gurkhas shared linguistic as well as cultural affinities with the Afghans. At a police post on the outskirts of Lashkar Gah, Rifleman Keshab Rai, 2d RGR, said that although he did not speak Pashto, the dominant language of southeastern Afghanistan, "We speak Urdu, and most of the people here speak Urdu."[29] The Gurkhas, recalled one British advisor, were "happy to carve up a goat and make a curry" to share with their Afghan counterparts. Moreover, their patience in dealing with the Afghans was remarkable, and beyond what most British soldiers were capable of providing, he said. Yet the police tried even the Gurkhas' considerable patience. The ANP's approach to its responsibilities was almost comically lackadaisical at times, as reflected in a press ac-

---

[29] "Gurkhas Train Afghan Police," UK Ministry of Defense, http://www.mod.uk/DefenceInternet/DefenceNews/MilitaryOperations/GurkhasTrainAfghanPolice.htm, accessed 2 March 2010. For more on the Royal Gurkha Rifles, see www.army.mod.uk/infantry/regiments/royal-gurkha-rifles/default.aspx, accessed 10 March 2010.

count of the arrival of an RGR police mentoring team at a checkpoint on Highway One, Lashkar Gah's main road.

> All of the policemen, except for the one guarding the main entrance, were found sleeping under a tent next to the road. . . . It took the Gurkhas nearly half an hour just to get everyone ready for that day's [training] session. Later that afternoon, the same British mentors stopped by another checkpoint where they found all 12 policemen at the post, including the commander, taking a postmeal nap.[30]

"It is hard to motivate the police," said one Gurkha officer. "Training them is not the hard part; teaching them discipline and determination is."[31]

Members of the Royal Gurkha Regiment look on as an Afghan policeman searches a resident in Musa Qala District.
(Crown Copyright/MOD 2008)

Conclusion

The experience of the British teams in and around Lashkar Gah illustrated some of the central challenges associated with police mentoring in Afghanistan. Like most other personnel advising the Afghans, they learned that the ANP was plagued by low morale, corruption, and a lack of discipline. These factors were formidable obstacles to building a cohesive, modestly competent force—let alone a professional law enforcement institution.

But, as the mentors discovered, it was important to do more than simply identify and lament the ANP's many shortcomings. The British came to recognize that making progress with the ANP required a strong measure of empathy—an obvious but essential quality when dealing with the Afghans.

---

[30] Anup Kaphle, "Policing Afghanistan," *The Atlantic*, September 2009, www.theatlantic.com/ magazine/archive/2009/09/policing-afghanistan/7685/, accessed 15 February 2010.

[31] Ibid.

The ANP, according to one officer, "were getting 'thumped' on behalf of the people," and they were also getting abused *by* the people—such as by local strongmen involved in narcotics trafficking. For policemen, like most other people in Afghanistan, scratching out an existence requires what in the Western context would be illicit, or at least questionable, survival skills. The quality of police recruits was poor, but this was partly a product of village-level destitution and the belief that physically and mentally feeble young men could make a career of policing.

In addition to empathy, police mentors needed patience—a quality that is sometimes in short supply among Western advisors in Afghanistan, who are typically eager to demonstrate near-term progress. The Gurkhas, who shared linguistic and cultural affinities with the Afghans, served a critical mentoring role, but even their patience was severely tested.

Vignette 4

Afghan National Civil Order
Police Advisor
2007–2008

A team made up of 16 members of the Michigan Army National Guard, led by a lieutenant colonel, arrived in Kabul in May 2007 expecting to advise an Afghan National Army (ANA) unit.[32] Instead, they were assigned to mentor the Afghan National Civil Order Police (ANCOP), a relatively new and specialized force, and spent a year doing so.

Afghan National Civil Order Police Roles and Missions

ANCOP was intended to function much like a European gendarmerie—that is, as a well-trained, disciplined paramilitary force capable of operating across the country. Its focus was on urban areas, and its men were trained to respond to riots and other forms of violent civil unrest, including hostage crises.[33] Indeed, ANCOP was established in response to the failure of the Afghan National Police (ANP) to quell violent protests in Kabul during mid-2006.

Recruits, who were drawn from the ranks of the ANP, received an additional 14 weeks of instruction, including specialized training in special weapons and tactics (SWAT) and

---

[32] Unless noted otherwise, quotations in this vignette are drawn from the author's telephone interview, 12 December 2010, and subsequent e-mail communications.

[33] "Afghanistan National Police Smartbook," CJTF-Phoenix J-3 Police Advisory Cell, 1 June 2007, 35. Combined Joint Task Force–Phoenix (CJTF-Phoenix), made up of personnel from 13 Coalition partner countries, mentors the ANA and ANP to improve their counterinsurgency and counterterrorism capabilities. CJTF-Phoenix is a subordinate command of the Combined Security Transition Command–Afghanistan (CSTC-A). CSTC-A's mission is to "plan, program and implement structural, organizational, institutional and management reforms of the Afghanistan National Security Forces in order to develop a stable Afghanistan, strengthen the rule of law, and deter and defeat terrorism within its borders." U.S. Navy, Expeditionary Combat Readiness Center, www.ecrc.navy.mil/1/idc_deployment/afghanistan.htm, accessed 2 March 2010. CSTC-A was brought under the command of NATO Training Mission–Afghanistan in 2009.

Members of the Afghan National Civil Order Police. (German Foreign Ministry photo)

crowd control.[34] Unlike the ANP—most of whom were illiterate—prospective ANCOP officers were required to possess basic literacy and numeracy skills.

In addition to riot control and other public order responsibilities, ANCOP was also expected to play a key role in an initiative to improve ANP training, discipline, and performance. Under the Focused District Development (FDD) program, uniformed police are removed from entire districts and sent to regional training centers. In their absence, ANCOP officers provide district-level security. Moreover, the relatively highly trained and motivated ANCOP personnel were intended to give an idea to local populations of how a professional police service should operate, and they were meant to set the bar against which returning local police would be judged.[35]

---

[34] Some of this training was provided by Germany and other NATO countries. "German Training for the Afghan Civil Order Police," www.diplo.de/diplo/en/Infoservice/Presse/ Meldungen/2008/080515-Afghanistan.html, accessed 22 January 2010.

[35] For more on FDD, see *Report on Progress toward Security and Stability in Afghanistan* (Washington, DC: Department of Defense, June 2008), 45; and Anthony H. Cordesman, Adam Mausner, and David Kasten, *Winning in Afghanistan: Creating Effective Afghan Security Forces* (Washington, DC: Center for Strategic and International Studies, May 2009), 106–11.

With most elements of the ANP, it was (and remains) impossible to determine the precise number of personnel at any given time. The ANP lacked a personnel accounting system and, moreover, local police chiefs kept significant numbers of no-show "ghost" policemen on the payroll.[36] In the case of ANCOP, however, the specialized nature of the force, its small size, and the relatively lavish amounts of attention paid to it by the United States and its international partners suggest that the published figure of 557 ANCOP officers (as of June 2007) was probably accurate.[37] Ultimately, the United States expected to increase the ANCOP force structure to 5,000 by the end of 2008.[38]

New Centurions

The police mentoring team (PMT) advised and trained ANCOP's 1st Brigade, headquartered in Kabul, and mentored ANCOP battalions in other provinces around Afghanistan. "My mentors went almost everywhere that our ANCOP guys went," the PMT commander recalled. With a team that eventually included more than 30 advisors, it was a rarity in Afghanistan, where most police advisory units have been considerably undermanned.[39] Nevertheless, mentors and other personnel remained in short supply. "We tried to assign one truck, three U.S. soldiers, and one interpreter to each ANCOP company, but we never had enough men to do so," the team leader said.

Like all ANCOP recruits, the men the PMT mentored had been through police basic training and had been vetted by the Afghan Ministry of Interior to screen out criminals and drug users. By Afghan police standards, the ANCOP officers were impressive, according to the team leader. Most were senior noncommissioned officers, and 85 to 90 percent

---

[36] Inspectors General, U.S. Department of State and U.S. Department of Defense (DOD), *Interagency Assessment of Afghanistan Police Training and Readiness* (Washington, DC: U.S. Department of State and DOD, November 2006), 11.

[37] "Afghan National Security Forces Order of Battle," *Long War Journal*, www.longwarjournal.org/oobafghanistan/index.php, accessed 10 March 2010.

[38] As of March 2010, there were a reported 4,900 ANCOP officers. T. Christian Miller, Mark Hosenball, and Ron Moreau, "The Gang That Couldn't Shoot Straight," *Newsweek*, 29 March 2010, www.newsweek.com/id/235221, accessed 22 March 2010.

[39] Inspector General, DOD, *Report on the Assessment of U.S. and Coalition Plans to Train, Equip, and Field the Afghan National Security Forces* (Washington, DC: DOD, 30 September 2009), 128. As of May 2009, only 2,375 mentors were in Afghanistan—just 39 percent of the requirement set by CSTC-A.

were literate. "Most could write Dari [the dominant language in the country's north and west] and some Pashto [dominant in the south and east]," recalled the PMT leader. As a national police force, the ANCOP was supposed to reflect the country's ethnic diversity, but "we seemed to be getting more Tajiks," he recalled.

In 2007–2008, centers used for ANCOP training were scattered around the capital—at the Kabul military training center, the ANP academy, and the ANCOP brigade headquarters. The dispersed nature of the training facilities meant that personnel had to be shuttled by bus between locations. This in turn created security problems. After a suicide bomber blew up one bus, "We changed bus colors," the team leader said, "and changed times so they [the insurgents] wouldn't know it was us."

The program of instruction focused almost exclusively on preparing the ANCOP for their public order duties. Training focused on groups of roughly 25 men. "We were not training them to be beat cops," according to the team leader. The focus was on riot and crowd control, SWAT, and other security missions. The mentors also instructed ANCOP personnel on how to establish and man "snap" traffic control points designed to apprehend a particular person or vehicle. Mentoring also included joint security patrols with ANCOP in and around Kabul.

SWAT training in Kabul, 2007.
(U.S. Department of Defense photo)

ANCOP officers typically met their mentors' expectations. "They did very, very well," stated the PMT leader. Particularly notable was the relative lack of corruption—a significant and enduring problem throughout the ANP.

"Sometimes they had their hands out with local merchants," said the team leader, "but they were basically not corrupt—they were like the 'New Centurions.'"

For instance, he recalled an incident where a local businessman was stopped by ANCOP officers because his car had illegal tinted windows. The businessman was stunned by the fact that ANCOP officers had not asked him for money—the standard operating procedure for the Afghan police in such circumstances.

All of the units that were mentored faced a very high operational tempo (OPTEMPO) in the field, and this high tempo limited the training the PMTs could provide. "OPTEMPO was our biggest enemy," the team chief recalled. "There was no time to do collective training, ordnance training, or maintenance training. There were multiple battalion operations all over the country all the time." The high tempo created an additional problem: with no time for official leave, police who wanted time off "would simply walk away, and some, but not most, would return," he said.

But overall, he judged the ANCOP's performance as good. A key metric of the ANCOP's professionalism was the opinion of village leaders during the FDD process, when local police were away at training centers. "Nine times out of ten, the locals would ask us to keep ANCOP there. They didn't want their sons and fathers back," said the PMT commander.

Conclusion

ANCOP was established as an elite national force that drew on relatively well-educated recruits and received longer and more sophisticated training than "conventional" Afghan police. As part of FDD, ANCOP was meant to fill in for district policemen who were receiving training at regional centers. Additionally, ANCOP was intended to serve as a model for professional policing by showing village residents how a competent and relatively uncorrupt force could serve the public. Ideally, the memory of ANCOP's positive performance would linger on as a yardstick for judging the post-FDD performance of the ANP.

The team commander's mentoring experience demonstrates that in at least one instance, the ANCOP was able to live up to U.S. and international partner expectations for the force. Although limited by a very high OPTEMPO, which reduced training time and contributed to desertions, the ANCOP mentored by the PMT appeared to be a reasonably disciplined and proficient force. While not incorruptible by Western standards, ANCOP officers were less predatory than typical Afghan police. Moreover, the fact that most village elders wanted ANCOP to remain confirmed to the commander that the force was of a far more professional caliber than the ANP it had replaced.

At the same time, it should be noted that ANCOP has not met with universal acclaim. ANCOP officers have performed professionally in many districts, but U.S. and British police mentors in southern Afghanistan have noted that after a few weeks in their assigned districts, ANCOP personnel would be suborned by local "strongmen" and engage in the same sorts of corruption and predation that characterized the ANP.[40]

Finally, U.S. and Coalition-force mentors have a "stiffening" effect on their Afghan counterparts. That is, the continuing Coalition presence probably helped foster ANCOP's relative success. It is uncertain whether the police will revert to their old corrupt and incompetent patterns once their patrons depart.

---

[40] Author's interviews with U.S. and UK police mentors, December 2009 and January 2010.

Vignette 5

Police Mentoring
Ghazni and Paktika Provinces, 2008–2009

A U.S. Army captain mentored Afghan National Police (ANP) units in southeastern Afghanistan from November 2008 to November 2009.[41] During the first eight months of his tour, he served in Ghazni Province. Police mentors under his command operated in five districts and 19 subdistricts. During his last four months in Afghanistan, he served in Paktika Province, where he mentored a variety of Afghan police units, including the Afghan Border Police (ABP).

Enhancing Highway Security in Ghazni

In addition to advising and training the ANP, the U.S. Army advisor worked with Afghan and Coalition forces, including the Poles, to secure a 140-kilometer (87-mile) stretch of Highway One. This highway, which is the central artery connecting Kabul and Kandahar, was the scene of frequent kidnappings and roadside bombings by the Taliban, as well as ordinary criminal activity, including truck hijackings and extortion.[42] The ANP, far from working to secure the highway, was responsible for some of the crimes on and around the road.

As the captain was struggling to bolster security, he was approached by a militia leader, a member of the Hazara ethnic minority, which throughout recent Afghan history had been marginalized politically and economically by the southern Pashtun tribes and north-

---

[41] Unless otherwise indicated, quotations are drawn from author's interviews with the U.S. Army captain mentioned in this vignette, Alexandria, VA, 4 and 16 December 2009 and 29 March 2010, and subsequent e-mail communications.

[42] See, for example, American Forces Press Service, "Coalition Forces Kill Taliban Fighters in Afghanistan," 29 December 2008, www.defense.gov/news/newsarticle.aspx?id=52498, accessed April 2010.

A vehicle search at a checkpoint in Ghazni Province, 2007. (U.S. Army photo)

ern Tajiks.[43] Operation Enduring Freedom and the collapse of the Taliban regime created new opportunities for the Hazaras, who saw cooperation with the Americans and their Coalition partners as an avenue out of isolation and oppression.

According to the army advisor, the militia leader was an influential man in southern Ghazni. He was widely respected for his daring exploits as an anti-Soviet mujahideen during the 1980s and had long been a player in local politics, having served as a subgovernor of two districts. The militia leader's first wife and son had been killed by the Taliban, and he was eager to work with the Americans. "He liked me because I was relatively powerful," the army advisor recalled. "I could call in F-15s." The quasi-official status occupied by the militia, while murky by Western standards, was not at all uncommon in the province—or in other regions of Afghanistan, for that matter. While tech-

---

[43] The ethnic composition of Afghanistan is Pashtun, 42%; Tajik, 27%; Hazara, 9%; Uzbek, 9%; Aimak, 4%; Turkmen, 3%; Baloch, 2%; and other, 4%. U.S. Central Intelligence Agency, *The World Factbook*, https://www.cia.gov/library/publications/the-world-factbook/geos/ af.html, accessed 5 April 2010.).

nically not police, the militia fighters acted like law enforcement officers. They wore ANP uniforms and were paid by the provincial governor to man four checkpoints along Highway One.

The militiamen established checkpoints at key places identified by the Americans. Locations used by foreign fighters were of particular importance. "I'd tell the leader, 'At this intersection where Uzbeks and Saudis are coming through, I want you to build a checkpoint,'" said the Army captain. The militia also served as a "force-multiplier" for the Afghan army and the ANP. The militiamen were frequently embroiled in firefights with the Taliban on and around the highway. "We would listen to the Taliban on our police scanner, and we knew they were fighting the militia," he recalled.

In exchange, the Americans supplied the militia with fuel. "We didn't pay them," the Army advisor said, "but we filled up their 55-gallon drums with gas so that they could move their little police force around." To put the force on a more professional footing, and to reduce opportunities for corruption, the captain got the governor to institute a direct-deposit system for paying the militiamen. In addition to concrete benefits, the militia received important intangible gains from their relationship with U.S. forces. "All they asked for was fuel, but they also got local prestige," declared the army advisor.

The Americans concluded that the militia was relatively effective in securing those stretches of the highway where they operated. It helped keep the Taliban off Highway One and ensure that commercial trucks got through. Moreover, unlike the ANP, the militia did not prey on the road traffic. "We polled truckers, and they said that militiamen were not stopping them," the captain recalled.

However, these gains proved to be temporary. The Americans later turned over responsibility for the artery to the Polish armed forces. By December 2009, Taliban activity and ordinary banditry was endemic along the entire length of the highway. "Under the Taliban regime," said a British Ministry of Defence spokesman, "you could put your daughter on a bus in Kabul, sure in the knowledge that she would get in one piece to Kandahar. That is not the case at the moment, and we need to change that."[44]

---

[44] Aislinn Laing and Ben Farmer, "Travelling by Road in Afghanistan 'Now More Dangerous than Under Taliban,'" *Daily Telegraph* (London), 4 December 2009, www.telegraph. co.uk/news/newstopics/politics/defence/6718217/Travelling-by-road-in-Afghanistan-nowmore dangerous-than-under-Taliban.html, accessed 5 April 2010.

Afghan Border Police in Paktika Province, 2009.
(U.S. Army photo)

The Afghan Border Police

During the final four months of his tour, the U.S. Army advisor served in western Paktika Province. There he oversaw the mentoring of the ANP as well as the ABP. The ABP mission was to provide security along international borders and at border crossing points; specifically, it was to prevent people and goods from illegally entering Afghanistan. It was also responsible for policing the "border security zone" that extended 50 kilometers (31 miles) from the international border into Afghanistan.[45] Finally, the ABP was assigned to collect tariffs and tolls, a potentially significant revenue source for the chronically cash-strapped Afghan central government.

According to the ANP's staffing structure (known as the *tashkeel*), the ABP had an authorized strength of 17,970 men.[46] However, this almost certainly did not reflect the actual number of ABP in service. As with other components of the ANP, it was next to impossible to determine how many members of the ABP were actually reporting for duty on any particular day, given the widespread presence of "ghost" policemen on the payroll and the lack of personnel-accounting systems.

Whatever the actual personnel numbers were, the ABP appeared incapable of performing its missions. Like much of the ANP, the border police was riddled with serious corruption. Taliban fighters and drug traffickers easily transited Afghanistan's long and porous borders, and large-scale smuggling was rampant.[47] Border control—a cornerstone of counterinsurgency theory and doctrine—was essentially nonexistent.

Border District Development

Shortly before the Army captain arrived in Afghanistan, the United States launched a major effort to build the ABP, which had received little American or NATO attention. Mod-

---

[45] "Afghan Border Police Undergoes Intensive Reform," *The Enduring Ledger* [Kabul, Afghanistan: CSTC-A], January 2009, 14.

[46] The authorized strength was inadequate, in the view of Gen Abdorrahman Rahman, the ABP commander, who insisted in April 2008 that 50,000 police were required. Trefor Moss, "Afghan Border Police Commander Warns on Personnel Shortage," *Jane's Defence Weekly* (online edition), 23 April 2008.

[47] United Nations, "Report of the Secretary-General on the Situation in Afghanistan and its Implications for International Peace and Security," UN Security Council and UN General Assembly, A/63/372-S/2008/617, 23 September 2008, 7.

eled on the Focused District Development program for the ANP, this pilot program in eastern and southeastern Afghanistan, known as Border District Development (BDD), planned to take 52 border police companies to regional centers for vetting, training, and re-equipping.

The Army advisor's involvement with the ABP began with the relatively modest task of ensuring that the border police, after training at the regional center in the town of Gardez in western Paktiya Province, were returned to their posts in the province's south on the Pakistan border. "Every two months, the ABP had a new training cycle, and a new graduating class that had to be moved," he recalled. There were two border posts in his area of responsibility, each manned by roughly 40 border police. The plan was to establish an additional three checkpoints and expand the total number of police in the area to 1,000.

During late 2008, the captain began pondering the fundamental problems associated with the border and their implications for developing the ABP. Known as the Durand Line, the border, set down in the nineteenth century to mark the boundary between Afghanistan and what was then British India, was merely that—a line on the map.[48] The formal Afghanistan-Pakistan frontier was simply ignored by insurgents, drug traffickers, and ordinary Pashtuns, who were spread across the border zone. "People thought nothing of moving across the border to visit family," recalled the captain.

Understanding the nature of this border zone was crucial, in his view. Too many Americans saw the border as controllable—a goal that was unattainable, he concluded. Instead of attempting to seal off and aggressively regulate the frontier—an aspiration that denied economic, social, and political reality—a priority should be to build a force capable of collecting tariffs for the government. In his judgment, the border-crossing points should be seen as "revenue-generating enterprises" manned by reasonable, professional police.

Like all units of the ANP, the border police were corrupt. But the advisor believed that there were different degrees of corruption and that corruption had different conse-

---

[48] The Durand Line has never been recognized by Afghanistan, which has long claimed Pashtun areas on Pakistan's side of the demarcation. Frédéric Grare, "Pakistan-Afghanistan Relations in the Post-9/11 Era," Carnegie Papers Number 72, Carnegie Endowment for International Peace, October 2006, 8.

quences. Shaking down the local population, plundering the ABP payroll, and selling weapons to the Taliban were examples of corruption that were institutionally and operationally destructive, and therefore unacceptable. On the other hand, selling gasoline provided by the United States, while hardly to be encouraged, represented a far lesser form of corruption—"a survival strategy, really," in his view.

Although prepared to tolerate relatively minor forms of graft, the captain believed that the border police could and should make progress over time. As he explained,

> We might expect them [the police] to work in all weather, and be fair and honest with everyone. But we need to understand that they will do things based on village, family, and tribal loyalties. We should expect for now that a border guard will let his father through without paying the tariff. But the corruption we accept today won't necessarily be acceptable in the future.

The advisor was committed to the notion that it was essential to build into the ABP policies and procedures that would reduce possibilities for corruption and would create positive patterns of behavior that would endure after the Americans left. For example, many officers were woefully underpaid; they would rob the local population to generate income. The captain helped ensure that the police were paid by direct deposit. ABP personnel were notified by their mobile phones that their pay had been deposited in a bank. The message he hoped to instill within the border police was, "I'm getting paid—now I should do my job right and not demand a portion of the tariff at the border crossing."

A border crossing in Kandahar Province. (U.S. Air Force photo)

During his four months of mentoring the ABP, he detected signs of progress. The BDD program was a step forward in his view. Before the initiative, border police "were just given a t-shirt and an AK-47 and told to man a post," he said. "Now, there is a vetted, trained force, and I think we were starting to get 'buy-in' from the ABP." This training, in his judgment, gave the ABP a better sense of unit cohesion and a greater ability to survive violent encounters with the Taliban.

During 2009, other U.S. officers noted greater professionalism among the ABP in Paktika Province. According to one press account, American personnel reported that recent graduates of the regional training center "not only look and act more polished, but are also more confident and motivated to protect their country."[49]

Conclusion

The Army captain's experiences during 2008 and 2009 illustrate three important and interrelated aspects of mentoring in Afghanistan. First, they show how junior commanders can exercise individual initiative and adapt successfully to complex local conditions. Faced with a persistently ineffectual ANP that was unable to provide security along the province's main highway, he looked beyond the official police and turned to an ethnic Hazara militia that was eager to work with U.S. forces.

Second, the advisor's tour highlights the often transitory and highly localized nature of improvements in the Afghan police and in security more generally. Security along the highway improved, but by the end of the year it had deteriorated again. Among the ABP in his area of responsibility, there were signs of greater professionalism and effectiveness. But these gains appeared to be local. On the whole, ABP professionalism and effectiveness was minimal, and corruption remained rampant, particularly in those areas where the police had access to commercial vehicles crossing the Afghan-Pakistan border.[50] Moreover, members of the ABP have reportedly engaged in cross-border smuggling—the very activity they are chartered to control.[51]

Finally, these experiences demonstrate the limits that any given mentor could be expected to achieve during his tour. Advisors had to grapple with the problems of police corruption, incompetence, and poor leadership. These maladies were formidable, but the mentors could have some reasonable hope that they could be ameliorated. Much more intractable was the nature of the border itself. Part of the challenge was the sheer length of the Afghan-Pakistan frontier, which stretches for roughly 2,600 kilometers (1,600 miles), much of it over extremely rugged and remote terrain. Human geography

---

[49] Soraya Sarhaddi Nelson, "Afghan Border Police Make Progress, Slowly," *National Public Radio*, 5 March 2009, www.npr.org/templates/story/story.php?storyId=101377415, accessed 2 April 2010.

[50] Anthony H. Cordesman, *Afghan National Security Forces: Shaping the Path to Victory* (Washington, DC: Center for Strategic and International Studies, 27 July 2009), 36.

[51] Matthieu Aikins, "The Master of Spin Boldak: Undercover with Afghanistan's Drug-Trafficking Border Police," *Harper's Magazine*, December 2009. On page 54 of this article, Abdul Razik, an ABP lieutenant, announced to a reporter that "I am a smuggler . . . I take cars and things to Pakistan."

also contributed to the problem of border control. Families and tribes had straddled the frontier for centuries and crossed it virtually at will. This reality frustrated any hope of establishing a strict border-control regime, as the captain concluded. Border security was rendered impossible by the actions of Afghanistan's neighbor to the east. For Pakistan, the border was a fiction that could be ignored in the interests of wider political objectives. As part of a wider campaign to influence events inside Afghanistan, Pakistan's intelligence services facilitated the movement of Taliban fighters across the frontier into Afghanistan.[52] Under such conditions, it seems safe to conclude that securing the border would have required much more than what police mentors could be expected to provide.

[52] Carlotta Gall, "Pakistan Accused of Backing Taliban," *New York Times*, www.nytimes.com/2007/01/21/world/asia/21iht-web.0121pakistan.FULL.4278465.html?_r=1, accessed 30 March 2010; and Matt Waldman, "The Sun in the Sky: The Relationship Between Pakistan's ISI and Afghan Insurgents," Crisis States Research Centre, London School of Economics and Political Science, Discussion Paper no. 18, June 2010.

Vignette 6

U.S. Marine Corps Police Mentoring Team Commander
Garmsir District, 2009

A first lieutenant in a military police (MP) company attached to the 5th Battalion, 10th Marines, arrived in Afghanistan in April 2009.[53] His 23-man platoon, which replaced a badly overstretched two-man contingent of British advisors, would spend the remainder of the year mentoring a group of policemen from Garmsir District in Helmand Province. His team spent the first two months with the Garmsir police at the regional training center in Spin Boldak District, Kandahar Province, and then returned with them to their home district to continue mentoring.

Police Shortfalls

Across Afghanistan, the U.S. approach to the Afghan National Police (ANP) stressed paramilitary rather than law enforcement training. Mentors typically stressed the development of tactical, battlefield skills rather than those used in preventing and investigating crime. This orientation was understandable, given that many mentors came from conventional infantry units.

As a Marine MP, the lieutenant brought a law enforcement perspective to his mentoring assignment. While acknowledging that the ANP needed skills for surviving violent encounters with the Taliban, he believed that the police also required more conventional law enforcement abilities that would enable them to protect the district's civilian population.

But the ANP was a long way from being able to provide anything approaching what the West refers to as "community policing." Widespread illiteracy among ANP officers was

---

[53] Unless otherwise indicated, quotations are drawn from the author's interviews with the mentoring team commander, Quantico, VA, 22 December 2009, and at Camp Lejeune, NC, 17 February 2010, and subsequent e-mail communications.

a particularly significant hurdle. "Paperwork, evidence, processing—they don't know how to do it," the lieutenant said. "You can't get a policeman to take a statement if he can't read and write."[54]

Moreover, the force was plagued by the other usual ills working against police professionalism and effectiveness in Afghanistan: physical disabilities, drug use, poor morale, and widespread corruption. Rather than providing law and order to the residents of Garmsir, the ANP in the district served as sources of insecurity.

A Marine police mentor conducts a class on search operations in Garmsir District, August 2009. (U.S. Marine Corps photo)

"We Were Always in Their Faces"

The lieutenant's approach to the ANP stressed "hands-on" mentoring. Under the Focused District Development (FDD) program, police from Garmsir and other districts were sent as units to regional training centers for an eight-week course, where they were trained, screened for drug use, and issued new uniforms and weapons. In their absence, members of the paramilitary Afghan National Civil Order Police (ANCOP) provided district security.

The Marine platoon commander concluded early in his tour that it was essential to attend the course along with the police he was mentoring. He and other members of his platoon stayed at the regional training center in Spin Boldak from April through mid-June. "We went through class with them," he recollected. "We were able to witness the training that the police received, and then hold them up to those standards after they graduated."

---

[54] Ann Scott Tyson, "Dearth of Capable Afghan Forces Complicates U.S. Mission in South," *Washington Post*, 25 July 2009, www.washingtonpost.com/wp-dyn/content/article/2009/07/24/AR2009072403760.html, accessed 23 October 2009.

An Afghan policeman at the regional training center in Kandahar.
(U.S. Air Force photo)

While the ANP was away, the citizens of Garmsir grew weary of ANCOP's paramilitary approach, confirming the platoon commander's belief that what the district needed was community-oriented policing. "They needed a sheriff, not riot control cops," he stated. So, despite the ANP's soiled reputation, district residents welcomed the return of the police. "They held a welcome-home parade for the ANP," he recalled.

The Marines' hands-on approach continued after the ANP's return to Garmsir. Rather than live at the forward operating base, the lieutenant decided to move his team into the local police station. "We were always in their faces," he said. The team routinely interacted with the ANP at meals and in chess games, darts, volleyball, and other diversions.

Such interactions were intended to foster a sense of camaraderie among the police and between the police and their mentors. To reinforce the instruction provided during FDD, the Marines also conducted follow-on classes in topics ranging from first aid to "cordon-and-knock" operations.

Patrolling with the Afghan National Police

Twice-daily patrols were a central part of the mentoring process. "It was important to show Afghans, not just tell them," said the platoon commander. Early in the morning, and again in the evening, three or four Marines and an interpreter would accompany a group of 10 to 15 Afghan police. "The police would hand out candy and drink tea with locals," he noted. "These security patrols were really community policing."

Police checkpoints were another focus of the mentors' attention. Many checkpoints were solid structures reinforced with sandbags and concertina wire. Typically, police lived as well as worked at their checkpoints.

In Garmsir, the police were reluctant to move from the relatively safe confines of the district center; living on their own at checkpoints would expose them to Taliban attacks. "We pressed them to move into checkpoints in outlying villages," remembered the lieutenant. "We wanted them to increase their influence in the villages and become the face of the government." Through regular visits from the mentors, including overnight stays, the ANP was persuaded to man the checkpoints.

Still, the police at checkpoints required careful monitoring and supervision. In addition to engaging in unprofessional behavior, such as napping on duty and taking drugs, the ANP used the checkpoints as platforms for extracting unofficial "tolls" and robbing vehicles and their passengers. Routine visits from the mentors were meant to deter crime

Marines prepare to patrol with the ANP in Garmsir District, August 2009.
(U.S. Marine Corps photo)

and dereliction. To ensure that the police were behaving properly, the mentors sometimes also conducted covert surveillance of the checkpoints.

During the summer, the MP platoon was joined by a civilian advisor working for a U.S. defense contractor. Since 2003, the contractor, under a series of contracts with the U.S. Department of State, had been responsible for setting up and running regional police training centers, providing logistical support to the Afghan police and a limited amount of training and mentoring outside the classroom setting.[55] At the regional training centers, Afghan nationals served as instructors but used a curriculum developed by the company.

Like other U.S. military personnel in Afghanistan, the Marines discovered that the company's field representatives varied widely in terms of their experience, expertise, and commitment. The first advisor sent by the contractor had to be replaced after he complained that conditions were "too Spartan," according to the lieutenant. His replacement arrived in August, about halfway through the platoon's tour.

A number of challenges emerged. The company claimed to have a thorough understanding of the Ministry of the Interior, the Afghan department responsible for equipping, paying, and supplying the ANP. But in the platoon commander's view, the contractor knew little about the Afghan support structure or how to exploit it for the benefit of the ANP. As a result, the ANP had to eke out whatever supplies and equipment it could. The mentors struggled to get the contractor to live up to its obligation to maintain the ANP's ramshackle fleet of Ford Ranger pickup trucks. "The ANP had to hitch rides from the locals. There was no logistics," he recalled.

He was also critical of the training that the contractor was responsible for providing at the regional training center. In his judgment, the company's program was inappropriate for the ANP. "It was unrealistic," the lieutenant proclaimed. "It focused on things like traffic policing and ethics, but it should have stressed community-oriented policing, conflict resolution, and dealing with the population." At his urging, the company modified the program of instruction, with less emphasis on lectures and more on practical policing demonstrations, such as how to conduct a search.

---

[55] As of January 2009, some 600 civilian police advisors—mostly from DynCorp—were working in Afghanistan. Kenneth Katzman, "Afghanistan: Post-War Governance, Security, and U.S. Policy," RL30588, Congressional Research Service, 16 January 2009, 38.

Signs of Progress

Over time, the platoon saw indications that the Garmsir ANP was improving. "They were paid attention to, given equipment, dressed like policemen and treated like policemen. So they started to act like policemen," the lieutenant said.[56] The FDD program was a key contributor to this growing professionalism, in his view. Attending the two-month course at the regional training center along with the ANP "set me up for success," he believes.

In addition to providing training and equipment, the FDD training strengthened bonds among the ANP, and between the ANP and their mentors. The district chief of police was willing to work with his American advisors. The chief was an influential man who was close to the district subgovernor. Be- cause of the Marines' good relationship with the district police chief, he could serve as a guide to the complex politics of policing in Garmsir.

The police advisors discovered that there were really two police forces in the district. In addition to the official ANP, there was an unofficial, "shadow" force run by a son of the former chief. The son considered the police to be a family business, and he believed that he had the right to inherit his father's post. In an effort to reduce tensions, the chief allowed the son to run some police checkpoints. The two men some- times worked together, but their rela- tionship remained strained.

Over the course of the summer and into the fall, the platoon detected signs

An Afghan policeman speaks with a village elder during a security patrol in Garmsir District, August 2009. (U.S. Marine Corps photo)

---

[56] Tom Coghlan, "Laying Down the Law: U.S. Tries to Make Policemen of the 'Robbers in Uniform,'" *The Times* (London), 21 July 2009, www.timesonline.co.uk/tol/news/world/asia/ article6721176.ece, accessed 12 February 2010.

of progress in the Garmsir police. The police chief showed increasing initiative. Instead of relying on the Marines to plan and schedule patrols, he took over responsibility for all phases of these missions. The chief also demonstrated a greater willingness to command. For example, he began holding twice-weekly group meetings with all of his checkpoint commanders.

According to the lieutenant, the ANP also showed improvement at the tactical level. In contrast to the ANP in other districts and provinces, the Garmsir police became something more than a paramilitary force: they developed elementary law enforcement skills, such as the ability to gather evidence and investigate crime, albeit in a rudimentary way.

Most significant from a counterinsurgency perspective was the apparently improving relationship between the ANP and the population they were meant to serve. Before the FDD training, local residents would never approach the police with information or complaints, but now they did, the platoon commander said. The stature of the police was increasing among the public who saw district police as an "emerging tribe" worthy of respect, according to the lieutenant. That said, by Western police standards, the Garmsir ANP could hardly be considered a model force. "They met the 'just good enough' criterion," the lieutenant concluded.

Conclusion

The emphasis that the platoon placed on building a public service-oriented police force in Garmsir was in contrast to the approach of many other police mentors in Afghanistan, who emphasized building ANP combat skills over law-enforcement training.

The public's greater willingness to share information with the ANP was likely a function of this new approach to policing as well as the police force's growing professionalism and discipline. That said, public support was hardly universal. In July 2009, one resident told a reporter, "People in Garmsir hate the police . . . [the police] just steal from the people and disturb the people."[57]

---

[57] Ibid.

The platoon's "hands-on" approach differed from that of other U.S. military mentors in Afghanistan. While some police advisors in other districts and provinces lived with the police, the lieutenant's decision to accompany the Garmsir ANP through its FDD training was unusual—and, in his judgment, it paid rich dividends in terms of building a relationship among the police and between the ANP and the mentors.

More typical were the Marine's challenges with the defense contractor responsible for supplying police advisors and other services. Across Afghanistan, U.S. military mentors have noted the varying degrees of expertise, experience, and motivation among defense contractors. Given the shortage of mentors, a lack of capacity within U.S. civilian agencies, and a long-term U.S. government policy that stresses contracting out many services, it seems inevitable that private companies will continue to play a role in building and supporting Afghanistan's security forces. As a result, many other mentoring teams will face the challenge of ensuring that contractors live up to their responsibilities.

Finally, the lieutenant's tour in Garmsir highlights other enduring challenges for police mentors. His mentoring team was at full strength, but elsewhere in Afghanistan police mentors were in short supply. Moreover, police forces across the country were significantly undermanned. In Garmsir, a mere 80 policemen were expected to serve a population of roughly 100,000 people.[58] To the extent that it helps create police forces that Afghans want to join, mentoring could spur recruitment.[59] However, a number of critical factors, such as low pay, are beyond the power of any individual police mentoring team to change.

---

[58] The population figure is from "Garmsir Returnees Angered at Devastation," Institute for War and Peace Reporting, 8 August 2008, http://www.iwpr.net/report-news/garmsir-returneesangered-devastation, accessed 10 April 2010.

[59] For Helmand as a whole, there were approximately 3,000 police for a population of roughly 1.4 million. "U.S. Boosts Effort to Train Afghan Police," National Public Radio, 27 May 2009, www.npr.org/templates/story/story.php?storyId=104607440, accessed 5 March 2010. The province's overall police-to-population ratio was better than it was in Garmsir, but still grossly inadequate by Western policing standards.

British Police Mentor
Helmand Province, 2009

A British Army lieutenant colonel arrived in Lashkar Gah, the capital of Helmand Province, in April 2009.[60] He spent his nine-month tour headquartered in the capital, where he served simultaneously in two mentoring roles: as the commander of British police mentors and as an advisor to the province's chief of police.

Mentoring the Afghan National Police

The lieutenant colonel's objective was to transform the province's roughly 2,400 members of the Afghan National Police (ANP) into what he termed "a disciplined body of men with professional policing skills." Building such a force would contribute to broader counterinsurgency goals. In his view, the police functioned as the "primary interface" between the public and the government. He believed that successful counterinsurgency required capable and credible state institutions, and that "if the police were not credible, the government wasn't credible."

Like the police in the country's other provinces, police in each district of Helmand Province were recruited locally.[61] Local recruits had a number of advantages, according to the British advisor. They had considerable knowledge about the people and conditions in their districts and did not pose the danger of exacerbating ethnic and tribal tensions the way recruits from outside of the area might. The problem for the mentors was that the province's recruitment pool was extremely shallow. Illiteracy, drug abuse, and corruption were rife; leadership skills were lacking; and across the province the ANP force was plagued with incompetence and unprofessionalism.

---

[60] Quotations in this vignette, unless otherwise noted, are taken from the author's interviews, Shrewsbury, UK, 6 February 2010, and subsequent e-mail communications.

[61] However, both the Afghan National Civil Order Police and the counternarcotics police were recruited on a national basis.

LtCol John E. McDonough, commanding officer of 2d Battalion, 2d Marines, speaks with LtCol Gul Aqa Amiry, the Garmsir Afghan Border Police commander, after a shura on 19 November 2009.
(U.S. Marine Corps photo)

Until a suitable local talent pool could be identified and nurtured, the logic of the situation dictated that the police look outside Helmand for individuals with leadership skills. But this was problematic. Police who were considered "foreigners" in local eyes could stir up communal conflict.

Moreover, capable police from outside the region had no desire to serve in Helmand's dangerous, insurgent-ridden environment. Like the ANP elsewhere in southern Afghanistan, the police in Helmand were used in offensive operations against the Taliban.[62] "Police in Kabul had no interest in giving up a safe job and going to Helmand," the UK mentor concluded.

The U.S. Marines Arrive

In early July 2009, the 2d Marine Expeditionary Brigade arrived in the province. The appearance of the Marines had a powerful impact on the ANP and their British mentors. The police, according to the lieutenant colonel, detected a shift in momentum in favor of the government, and the ANP "realized that the Taliban were not going to regain power" in Helmand.

Before the Marines arrived, he recalled, "The police were willing to switch sides and join the Taliban." Now, for the first time in modern memory, serving in the ANP became a "viable, long-term choice for the Afghans," said the police advisor. Similarly, the arrival of the Marines reinforced his belief that the tide had turned against the Taliban and the long-term prospects for the ANP were good: "I was convinced that the UK and the Marines could create a disciplined body of men."

---

[62] Policing in Afghanistan was a high-risk occupation. "Between January 2007 and October 2008, international forces suffered 464 personnel killed in action, the ANA lost 505 personnel, and the ANP lost 1,215." DOD, *Report on Progress Toward Security and Stability in Afghanistan* (Washington, DC: DOD, June 2009), 32.

Afghan police at the Helmand police training center in Lashkar Gah in January 2010.
(U.S. Air Force photo)

Training for the police grew more rigorous and systematic over the course of the summer. Previously, Afghan policemen "had simply been given a gun and told to go to a checkpoint," the British advisor recalled. The ANP in selected districts, under the Focused District Development program, were now being sent to training facilities, where they were screened for drug use, re-equipped, and given instruction in basic skills. "Now they had to meet pass-out requirements, and only at that stage could they go to checkpoints," he noted.

The Marine presence improved security in the province. Rather than fight the Taliban, the ANP could now focus on serving the local population. Greater professionalism among the police was instilling growing confidence in the province's residents. "The population has proven to be quite content to ring up and pass on information," the British mentor said.[63] Still, the ANP had not reached Western law enforcement standards and had

[63] Ben Glaze, "Anglesey Soldier's Taxing Question to Brown," WalesOnline, 30 August 2009, www.walesonline.co.uk/news/wales-news/2009/08/30/anglesey-soldier-s-taxing-question-to-brown-91466-24563479/, accessed 5 March 2010.

a long way to go. The police, he said, were not yet conducting "what you and I would call community policing."[64] But, in his view, "conditions were being set for success."

Taliban Administration

During his tour in Helmand, the lieutenant colonel developed an understanding of the Taliban's formidable ability to exercise control over villages and districts in the province. According to him, the Taliban were made up of three elements: the "hard-core" fighters; the foreign or "out-of-area" fighters—including Uzbeks and Pakistanis—who supplied important technical skills, such as those for making improvised explosive devices; and local insurgents, who made up the vast majority of fighters.

---

[64] Ibid.

A Tribal shura in Helmand Province in July 2009. (U.S. Marine Corps photo)

In the police advisor's view, the hard-core fighters and foreign fighters were irreconcil-able and had to be defeated with force. Local fighters, on the other hand, could and should be won over. Many of them, he concluded, were "ten-dollar Taliban" who simply saw the conflict as a means to survive. "War was a way of life to them," he concluded. "They had fighting skills, which were a way to get food."

But the Taliban did more than fight—they also provided local residents with critical serv-ices that the Afghan government was unable to deliver. In particular, the Taliban ad-dressed the security gap experienced by most of the population. "The fundamental thing an Afghan wants is to get up in the morning knowing he can work his fields, take his produce to market without being intimidated by the Taliban or the police, and return home knowing he will find his family safe," said the British mentor.

Bashran, a district north of Lashkar Gah, offered an example of what the Taliban could deliver. From their courthouse, the Taliban dispensed informal justice. Tribal elders, who had traditionally provided justice, had been driven out of the district and replaced with the Taliban's own local people. "The Taliban demonstrated the higher level of se-curity they could provide," the UK advisor recalled. The Taliban also conducted their own reconstruction and development activities. Bazaars were open, and the economy was vibrant. "It outpaced anything we were able to do," he declared. "Shadow govern-ment is easy for the Taliban. They didn't do everything, and any shortfalls could be blamed on the government."[65]

Informal Justice

For the lieutenant colonel, justice administered informally at the village level needed to be a part of security sector reform in Afghanistan. Customary or traditional justice had been a feature of local life for centuries. Its effectiveness and legitimacy stemmed from the fact that it was provided locally by respected figures. The Taliban accepted these tra-ditional, informal means—albeit with their own, handpicked figures in charge.

Reflecting a long history of administering an empire indirectly through tribal and other elites, the British also recognized the importance of Afghanistan's traditional justice

---

[65] According to the British advisor, the Afghan government—unlike the Taliban—was attempting to set up an education system. "Education was something local communities desperately wanted," he said. In his view, education should be highlighted as a "defining benefit" to the population for supporting the government rather than the insurgents.

system. At the same time, they stressed the need to integrate the customary institutions into the country's formal justice system.

Toward that end, the British-led provincial reconstruction team in Helmand supported prisoner-review shuras.[66] Established in the districts of Musa Qala, Sangin, and Nad-e-Ali, these mechanisms were traditional in many respects, but they were also a part of Afghanistan's formal justice structure. In the words of one analyst, the prisoner-review shuras helped "prevent excessive prisoner detention, and ensure[d] the release of prisoners with no evidence against them . . . [They were] also integrated into the formal justice sector, with serious cases transferred to Lashkar Gah and the central rule of law system."[67] In the British mentor's view, these shuras reflected Afghan history and culture while acknowledging that "the formal justice system still had to exist, and murderers had to go to prison."

Village Self-Defense Forces

The British mentor also believed that an American program to create local self-defense forces had to include provisions for making these forces part of the country's official security structure. Known as the Community Defense Initiative, the program used U.S. Special Forces in a small number of areas around the country to help villagers organize to defend themselves against the Taliban.[68]

---

[66] Based in Lashkar Gah, the provincial reconstruction team was a component of Task Force Helmand, a primarily British force that also included a Danish battle group as well as Polish and Czech contingents.

[67] Andrew Legon, "Ineffective, Unprofessional, and Corrupt: The Afghan National Police Challenge," Foreign Policy Research Institute, June 2009, www.fpri.org/enotes/200906.legon.afghannationalpolice.html, accessed 25 April 2010. According to the UK Foreign and Commonwealth Office, the prisoner review shuras "represent an intersection between the formal and informal justice sectors in that they use a traditional forum (the shura) while involving the statutory agencies (Afghan National Army, Afghan National Police, National Directorate of Security), as well as community representatives where elected." "Written Evidence Submitted by the Foreign and Commonwealth Office: London Conference Update," 18 February 2010, www.publications.parliament.uk/pa/cm200910/cmselect/cmfaff/398/398we03.htm, accessed 20 April 2010.

[68] For more on the history of village self-defense, see Seth G. Jones, "Community Defense in Afghanistan," *Joint Forces Quarterly*, no. 57 (2010).

Afghan police at a checkpoint with a British advisor in Sangin.
(Photo courtesy of Andre Prudent)

The lieutenant colonel was skeptical about the program at first. He knew of at least one case where members of local defense forces were not being paid and were accountable only to the village elders. "The last thing you needed was a group of armed civilians running around," the UK advisor said. "There were tribal disputes daily, and it was very easy for them to escalate. Without salaries they would have to steal from the very community they were supposed to be protecting." In one village in Helmand, U.S. commanders were convinced that the village defense force should be given uniforms, receive a salary, and become a part of the ANP. "They became accountable," he stated, adding that becoming part of the country's formal security structure "gave them tremendous pride."

The Provincial Chief of Police

Much of the lieutenant colonel's tour was occupied with mentoring the provincial chief of police. Like a number of other senior Afghan security officials, the police chief had been trained by the Russians and had survived decades of war in the province. He had considerable leadership talent, and he was determined to reform the ANP. "He had strength of will, and he was capable of delivering in the short term," the UK advisor recalled. "He understood that his political survival depended on improving the capability and credibility of the ANP."

Mentoring the police chief, like mentoring all of the police, required considerable patience as well as an ability to overcome an understandable desire to accomplish as much as possible during a relatively short tour. Avoiding the "'fix it, and fix it yesterday' mentality" was crucial, in the UK advisor's judgment. A police mentor, he believes, should focus "not on what I can do, but what I can do for the next guy."

Effective mentoring also required an understanding of Afghan culture. "Afghanistan is a warrior society," he said, "and they want their mentors to look the part." Toward that end, he took care to ensure that both his appearance and bearing were always highly professional. "You are a status symbol, and you can enhance the credibility of the people you mentor," he said.

He took additional steps that reinforced the police chief's position and prestige. On one occasion, the chief "rang up and told me that a checkpoint was under attack, and asked me what I was going to do about it. I was able to divert an Apache [helicopter] and keep the checkpoint from being overrun. The police chief got a huge boost of credibility with his men."

Success required both empathy and a sensitivity to the human dimension of mentoring. As he noted: "It was about personal relationships, mutual respect, and not being arrogant. It was really about good manners." Trust was important, but it had limits. "The Taliban had plants in the ANP, and you had to keep an eye open," the UK advisor explained. "Partnership doesn't mean complete trust, but rather the appearance of complete trust," he added.

Successful mentoring also required a willingness and ability to let the Afghans fail—and learn from the experience, according to the lieutenant colonel. He remembered one incident when the Ministry of Interior insisted on sending 150 policemen for training in Ghorak District in Kandahar Province:

> We had no way to get them there, no way to validate the training, and the time line was all wrong. We were opposed, but they went through with it anyway. Needless to say, it was a complete failure with no training actually taking place, and they were stuck for three weeks trying to get back. We let them make the decision, but we made it clear where we stood, and they finally started to appreciate the level of planning detail required.

In his view, the successful mentors were the ones who realized that "one day the Afghans would have to stand on their own."

Conclusion

The British advisor's tour in Helmand illustrates important dimensions of police mentoring in Afghanistan. His goal was to build a disciplined, professional force, but the quality of locally recruited personnel was poor. Looking outside the province for higher-quality men was also problematic: suitable outsiders were less knowledgeable about local conditions; their presence could cause communal tensions; and they were unlikely to be willing to serve in Helmand's violent environment.

Like the ANP in much of Afghanistan, the police force in Helmand was riddled with corruption, incompetence, and drug abuse. Moreover, its loyalty was very much in doubt. In the view of the lieutenant colonel, the arrival of the U.S. Marines in July 2009 helped convince the police that the Taliban could not prevail and that being part of the ANP was a "viable, long-term choice."

The UK advisor's experience with the province's chief of police highlights the significance of mentoring's intangible aspects. He believed that successful mentoring in Afghanistan's "warrior culture" required him to capitalize on his own status as a member of the profession of arms. He used his own professional military bearing and performance to bolster the police chief's prestige among his men and his colleagues.

The lieutenant colonel's tour also gave him insights into the Taliban. He observed the movement's program to control populations in the province and noted its ability to "out-compete" the Afghan government in terms of providing local security and development.

Finally, the British advisor's experience illustrates some of the complexities surrounding efforts by Coalition forces to address the gaps in security and justice created by the lack of Afghan government capacity. Initiating prisoner-review shuras and building village self-defense forces were two attempts to build on long-standing local mechanisms to provide critical public services. But in the UK mentor's view, their contribution to long-term success in counterinsurgency required them to be linked to Afghanistan's official justice and security system.

Regional Police Mentoring
Team Commander
Northern Afghanistan, 2007–2008

Arriving in Mazar-e Sharif, Balkh Province in May 2007, a colonel in the Iowa Army National Guard spent the next 12 months serving as the commander of a regional police advisory team.[69] An infantry officer who in civilian life worked for a manufacturing company, the colonel had expected to mentor units of the Afghan National Army (ANA). But shortly before arriving in Afghanistan he was ordered to work with the Afghan National Police (ANP).

Although relatively peaceful when compared to other parts of the country, his area of responsibility in northern Afghanistan was vast. With a population of approximately 9 million, it included nine provinces that stretched 1,200 kilometers (747 miles), from Faryab in the west to Badakshan in the east.[70] The deficiencies of the region's 11,000 police were profound: corruption, a lack of public respect and trust, poor leadership, and widespread illiteracy. Moreover, the police at all levels were plagued by a lack of organization, poor logistics, and vast shortages of equipment. The colonel had two primary tasks: advising the Afghan police chief responsible for the northern region and commanding police mentoring teams (PMTs) who served at the provincial and district levels. He also provided a limited amount of mentoring to the Afghan Border Police. "We weren't resourced for it, but I tried to spend time with the border brigades," he said.

Mentoring the Regional Police Chief

The guidance the PMT commander received from higher headquarters identified five

---

[69] Unless otherwise indicated, quotations are drawn from the author's interview, National Harbor, MD, 18 November 2009.

[70] However, during this period, mentoring took place in only eight out of nine provinces. Badakshan, a low-priority province, was excluded.

functional areas requiring particular attention by mentors at all levels: personnel, training, finance, logistics, and operations. As the mentor to the regional police chief, the advisor focused on building staff skills and, more broadly, injecting a measure of U.S.-style military rationality into the administration and organization of the region's policing structure.

The regional chief, a two-star Afghan police general, was a promising subject for mentoring, in the advisor's view: "He was a career police officer, very professional, and literate in Dari." But the staffing structure in place was highly inefficient by U.S. standards. For example, three to five people would be responsible for one area of logistics: "one

for weapons and ammo, one for food, and so on, with all of them reporting to the chief of police." The mentor instituted an American-style staff structure, with one individual responsible for operations, one for pay, and one for logistics.

He also encouraged the regional chief to assert his authority over his provincial police commanders. Although the regional chief was nominally in charge, the provincial chiefs were appointed by the Ministry of Interior (MoI)

Police training, Mazar-e Sharif regional training center in January 2007. (U.S. Army photo)

and, ultimately, the Afghan president, and they treated their provinces as independent fiefdoms. "The nine province chiefs were supposed to report to him, but they went around him and dealt directly with the MoI in Kabul," recalled the colonel.

Some had spent as much as $400,000 to "buy" their positions from the authorities in Kabul, according to the mentoring team commander. Much of the police leadership at the provincial level was rife with corruption. "The Kunduz chief of police was the most corrupt," he remembered. This chief controlled a bridge to Tajikistan, and he was able to extract revenues from the cross-border trade. Members of the Afghan security forces fought openly for control of the bridge and its revenues. "There were running gun battles, with the ANA sometimes fighting the ANP," the colonel recalled.

At the advisor's urging, the regional chief assembled the nine provincial commanders. "He got them all together and told them he'd go to the MoI and get them what they needed," the colonel said. But while the Americans detected some signs of progress, the regional chief could ultimately do little to reign in individuals who had direct relationships with senior figures in Kabul.

Local Police Mentoring

At the district level, the immediate need according to the mentor was to improve "tactical, day-to-day police operations." Many police did little more than guard their stations or man highway checkpoints—typically mud brick structures or shipping containers—and collect unofficial "tolls." In some instances, weapons were not even distributed. "The chief of police kept them [locked up] in a magazine," he said. "If things went bad, he could use them to start his own militia."

Police at the district level were also plagued by shortages of uniforms, blankets, food, and other materiel and equipment. These scarcities could be attributed largely to pervasive corruption, but the colonel thought that the lack of organization, procedures, and discipline also played a part. He related an incident in fall 2007, when mentors were helping the police in one province prepare for winter:

> We helped them put together a request to the MoI for warm clothes. They were shipped in multiple Connex [shipping] containers down to provincial headquarters. We worked with headquarters to distribute them to 11 or 12 districts. But when the containers arrived in a district, all of the police showed up at the same time and there was a mad scramble around the containers. There were brawls over the clothes and blankets.

The PMTs under the colonel's command were considerably understrength. "They were supposed to have 16 men, but they usually only had 9 or 10," he said. In addition to officers and senior noncommissioned officers, the teams included personnel from a U.S. contractor that provided trainers (typically retired law enforcement officers) for police advisory missions.

The quality of the contract advisors varied, according to the PMT commander: "Some were very experienced, with 25 years as sheriffs, but many only had two or three years of law enforcement experience." The nature of their experience also varied. "You could have a 'good old boy' from a small town who had been writing tickets for barking dogs," he recollected.

Under the Focused District Development program, police were sent from their districts for eight weeks of instruction at regional training centers in Kunduz and Mazar-e Sharif. After their return to their home villages, they were to be mentored by PMTs.

Field operations, which were part of the mentoring effort, proved to be a challenge for the ANP. Working with the U.S. and NATO forces, the ANA would set up an outer security cordon around a village. A police commander would then meet with town notables in order to ask permission to search houses for weapons caches. As part of the operation, Afghan and Coalition personnel would perform "medical civic action"—that is, establish temporary clinics and provide local communities with basic treatment in an effort to build popular support for the Afghan government.[71]

After a few days, the military forces would leave, and the ANP would remain in the village. The problem was that the police lacked the resources to stay for extended periods. "The ANP isn't expeditionary," the police mentor said. "They didn't have the food, bedding, or fuel. They just couldn't sustain themselves."

International Partners and the Afghan Police

The U.S. Army was not the only force mentoring police in northern Afghanistan. A variety of European countries and organizations carried out separate but overlapping police training activities.

---

[71] For more on medical civic action, see Frank J. Newton, "Medical Civic Action Programs for the 21st Century: The Application of Military Medicine in Civil-Military Operations," www.apmmc.org/2010-presentations/Thursday/Breakout4_Java/Newton.pdf, accessed 5 December 2010.

Police training teams from Coalition partner countries were assigned to their respective provincial reconstruction teams (PRTs).[72] These teams trained local Afghan police in criminal investigation, traffic control, administration, and other law enforcement skills. The European Union Police Mission in Afghanistan (EUPOL)[73] focused on building police institutions at the provincial and regional levels. EUPOL advisors worked at provincial police headquarters, at the MoI in Kabul, and as members of their national PRTs. A separate German Police Project Team supplied equipment; built infrastructure; and trained the Afghan National Civil Order Police, the ANP's specialized riot-control force.

This complex array of international police advisors created challenges for the advisor. "I probably spent more time working with the Coalition than with the ANP," the colonel recalled. With PRTs, EUPOL, and the Germans pursuing different and sometimes competing agendas, he attempted to synchronize the multinational effort. "I'd meet once a week with the German provost marshals," he said. Some issues involved the lack of resources—the Swedish PRT, for example, was chronically underfunded, and so had difficulty carrying out effective mentoring.

A U.S. Army mentor and an Afghan police officer examine an improvised explosive device during an operation in Faryab Province, November 2007.
(U.S. Navy photo)

---

[72] The PRTs were under the command of the ISAF, the NATO-led force established by the UN Security Council in December 2001.

[73] For more on EUPOL, see "EUPOL Afghanistan: European Union Police Mission in Afghanistan," www.eupol-afg.eu/, accessed 6 December 2010.

A European Union Police Mission in Afghanistan officer mentors the Afghan National Police.
(EUPOL photo)

The more fundamental issue was one of policing philosophy. These different views were irreconcilable. In the colonel's judgment, the ANP needed paramilitary rather than law enforcement training. "Afghanistan needed a force that could provide security," he remarked. "It was like the Wild West in the 1860s, and the police needed combat skills to survive."

The Europeans, however, stressed the need to build forces for civilian policing rather than counterinsurgency missions.[74] The Finnish/Swedish PRT in Mazar-e Sharif "trained the ANP in CSI [crime scene investigation] and chain of custody," the PMT commander recalled. The Norwegian PRT in Faryab Province had a more appropriate approach, he said, "but they didn't understand why the police needed machine guns and RPGs [rocket-propelled grenades]."

---

[74] As noted in a UK parliamentary report, "The U.S. and NATO's prime concern was rapidly to build an anti-insurgency force where numbers and speed were important, using a basic six-week NTM-A [NATO Training Mission–Afghanistan] training course (which mainly covered the use of firearms). EUPOL on the other hand aimed to form a force, which would undertake a traditional policing role over the longer term." House of Lords, European Union Committee, *The EU's Afghan Police Training Mission*, 8th Report of Session 2010–11 (London: The Stationery Office Limited, 16 February 2011), 23.

Ultimately, the disagreement between the advisor and the other international mentors was a product of the failure of the United States and the Coalition forces to make a first-order decision about the ANP's roles, missions, and functions—specifically, whether the force should support counterinsurgency operations or serve as a conventional law enforcement service.

Police Mentoring Lessons

The colonel arrived in Afghanistan after two months of mentor training at Fort Riley, Kansas. That instruction focused on practical skills, such as convoy operations, as well as Afghan cultural awareness and a smattering of language classes. But he said he received no training in how to actually mentor Afghans. "There was nothing on how to mentor," he recalled.

Acquiring mentoring skills required on-the-job training. Successful mentoring, in his judgment, had to be built on a foundation of personal relationships. "You can be a highly proficient officer, but if you can't develop relationships, the Afghans tune you out," he noted. One of the most effective PMT members was a first lieutenant who served as a firefighter in civilian life: "He was very engaging, and he developed great relationships with senior officers," recollected the colonel.

Negotiation, compromise, and a willingness to commit vast amounts of time to nurturing the Afghan personnel were essential, in his view. It took at least three or four long visits with a counterpart before a mentor could begin to build a relationship. "On the first visit you have to spend a few hours talking about things in general," according to the commander. "You have to let them talk. If you let them talk, they will eventually come around and recognize the right thing to do." After a relationship was established, it was possible to give advice more explicitly. He believed that the ability to provide guidance—not just impart technical skills—was the ultimate measure of effective mentoring.

Conclusion

The colonel's tour in northern Afghanistan highlights the complexities of the environment in which police mentors operated. His predeployment training did little to help him understand the demands he would face. By Western military standards, command and control arrangements were irrational and inefficient. The regional chief of police exercised only nominal control over his provincial subordinates, who retained independent relationships with the MoI in Kabul—the true center of power.

Corruption among senior ANP officials in some provinces reached truly industrial proportions. Police chiefs "bought" their positions from senior officials in the capital, and they used their positions to further criminal enterprises.

The ANP's logistical and materiel shortfalls were daunting. At the most fundamental level, the ANP lacked the organization and structure to keep its officers fed, clothed, and equipped. After joint operations in remote areas with U.S., NATO, and Afghan army forces, the ANP was expected to remain behind and provide police projection—a goal thwarted by the lack of the ANP's "expeditionary" capability.

Adding to the complexity was the presence of an array of police mentors drawn from Coalition partners and multinational bodies, such as the European Union. Synchronizing the efforts of actors who had overlapping agendas proved to be a considerable challenge. Some of these mentors, such as those in the Swedish PRT, were lacking in resources and thus limited in their ability to contribute to the broader police training effort in the region.

Nevertheless, the most fundamental obstacle was a difference in policing philosophies. Although the northern region was among Afghanistan's safest areas, the PMT commander maintained that mentoring should stress paramilitary "survival" skills. European mentors, on the other hand, insisted on the primacy of improving the ANP's policing skills, including criminal investigation, traffic control, and administration.

As one leading authority on the Afghan police has concluded, the Europeans typically "stressed the importance of community policing and taught civilian police skills, but they also reflected differing national policing philosophies and practices, adding another level of confusion to an already bifurcated program."[75]

---

[75] Robert M. Perito, "Afghanistan's Police: The Weak Link in Security Sector Reform," U.S. Institute of Peace, Special Report 227, August 2009, 11.

Ultimately, the difference in policing philosophies stemmed from the failure of the United States and the Coalition forces to make a first-order decision about whether the ANP's role was to support counterinsurgency operations or to serve as a conventional law-enforcement service.

U.S. Marine Corps Police Mentoring Team Commander
Nawa-I-Barakzayi District, 2009

A U.S. Marine staff sergeant serving in a military police (MP) company, 2d Marine Division, arrived in Nawa-I-Barakzayi District, Helmand Province, in May 2009.[76] During his seven-month tour, he led a police mentoring team (PMT). During that time, he advised groups of Afghan National Police (ANP) officers, as well as the district's chief of police.

The District's Police

The sergeant arrived in Afghanistan expecting to perform conventional MP roles and missions in a combat environment—such as main supply route clearance and convoy security. Instead, he was attached to the 1st Battalion, 5th Marines, and in June was sent as part of a four-man advance party to Nawa to prepare for the arrival of the main body of the PMT.

The 23-man team began its work with the ANP in July. Police deficiencies in the district were considerable. Few residents volunteered for the ANP. Village elders, under pressure from district and provincial officials, offered up recruits, but these men were typically drawn from the bottom strata of village life. The vast majority of the district's police were uneducated, malnutrition was widespread, and some policemen "were physically and mentally challenged," according to the sergeant.

Lawlessness among the police was rampant. "We had reports on the ANP—drugs, illegal taxation, and corruption," the PMT leader recalled. "Eighty percent of the police were high on drugs, and 50 percent of this drug use involved opiates," he said. The ANP also routinely "shook down" Afghan civilians, he added, "and if they didn't have the money, the police would kidnap family members for ransom."

---

[76] Quotations used in this vignette are drawn from the author's interview with the mentoring team commander, Camp Lejeune, NC, 17 February 2010, and subsequent e-mail communications.

Dried poppy in Nawa-I-Barakzayl District (U.S. Marine Corps photo)

"Spinning Them Up"

The immediate challenge was to prepare Nawa's police for the Focused District Development (FDD) program. Under FDD, an entire district's force was sent through a six-week course at a regional training center (RTC), where they were vetted, trained, given new uniforms and identification cards, and then returned to their home district, where they received follow-on mentoring.[77]

Before the police were sent to the RTC, American personnel screened them for drug use. Marijuana was tolerated, but any evidence of opiate use was grounds for exclusion from the training course. Moreover, the PMT encouraged the Afghans to fire any ANP member who tested positive for opiates. "We couldn't fire them, but we did pressure the Afghans to get rid of them," remarked the sergeant.

---

[77] In their absence, the Afghan National Civil Order Police provided district security. The course was originally eight weeks long, but was subsequently shortened to six weeks in order to speed up the FDD process.

For the remainder of the summer, the team focused on improving the ANP's skills—"spinning them up technically and tactically," in his words. Progress was slow. "Everything was so basic," he said. Lectures and formal classes were out of the question as the Afghans found it difficult to pay attention for extended periods of time. Instead, the Marines had to "schedule fun," he recalled. "We did things like room clearing—the Afghans weren't proficient, but it would hold their attention."

Mentoring by Example

The PMT also sought to improve the moral caliber of Nawa's police. They "had to be taught how to be decent human beings first—we couldn't just teach a bunch of thugs better skills," noted the sergeant. Building relationships with the Afghans was a critical step. Showing an interest in their life stories and their families, and understanding police officers on a personal level "helped us gain influence," he recalled.

Team members attempted to teach by example. Professionalism, respect, and discipline among the Marines, the PMT commander thought, would help improve the outlook and performance of the ANP. The PMT worked to instill in the Afghans the notion that policing was a worthy cause and that "there was honor in protecting someone."

The sergeant stressed the need for firmness in dealing with the Afghans. While showing that they cared about ANP officers on a personal level, the trainers also expected the police to live up to standards. "We wouldn't accept excuses like 'my foot hurts,'" he recalled. "At first we were worried about offending them, but then we learned that if you're soft, they won't respond."

Training at the Regional Training Center

In October, Nawa District's police force was sent off to the RTC in Kandahar. Members of the team accompanied the ANP throughout the six-week course. Going with the Nawa police allowed the Marines to judge the caliber of the training that the police received at the training center. PMT members also mentored the Afghan personnel who provided the instruction. "We were there as quality control for the Afghan instructors," the team leader said.

A U.S. Army mentor oversees Afghan policemen at the Kandahar regional training center.
(U.S. Air Force photo)

Training at the RTC stressed combat and survival skills, including mounted patrols, movement to contact, fire and maneuver, and improvised explosive device (IED) awareness. In the sergeant's judgment, the training's heavily military orientation was essential. In his view, the first priority had to be turning the Nawa ANP into a disciplined force—and that required military training. "They had no focus on discipline," he said. "They needed to be stripped of civilian habits and built up as professionals." Training in police-specific skills could come later, he said.

The team accompanied 172 Nawa policemen to the RTC. A handful deserted while on the course, and a number left because of medical problems. A total of 160 passed the program and returned to their district.

The six-week course in Kandahar had a positive effect on the Nawa police. They returned to the district with a new sense of pride. "They were more confident," the PMT commander recalled. With new uniforms and new equipment, including body armor, the policemen "were walking tall." But this progress was limited. In such skills as room clearing and movement to contact, the ANP showed no improvement. "Post-RTC, they were no better tactically," he concluded.

Reports from district residents suggested that police corruption also declined after the FDD training. But in the PMT commander's view, this was a result of the Marines' watchful presence in the district rather than any fundamental improvement in the ANP's ethics.

Mentoring the District Chief of Police

In addition to training and advising the Nawa ANP, the PMT leader also mentored the district's chief of police. "I spent every other day with him," the sergeant recalled. The district chief was a poor leader in the sergeant's judgment: "He didn't care about training or about anyone other than himself and his inner circle. He never asked for blankets or pots and pans for his men." Moreover, the district chief had a difficult relationship with the province's widely respected chief of police.[78]

Like the Marine advisor, the provincial police chief was unhappy with the district police chief's performance. According to the sergeant, the district chief "had been surrounded by the Taliban for 14 months," and it was widely believed that during that time he had "made a deal" with the insurgents. He had also alienated the district's population, who considered him "uncooperative," according to the Marine mentor.

---

[78] See vignette 7 for more on the provincial police chief.

In August 2009, the provincial police chief sent a group of 50 Afghan policemen from Lashkar Gah, the provincial capital, to Nawa, ostensibly to provide security for upcoming presidential elections. The sergeant suspected that the real reason they were sent was to improve the public's perception of the ANP. The Nawa District police chief had neglected his own men, and he had also ignored the security concerns of district residents. "It was a 'hearts and minds' effort," said the Marine.

A U.S. Marine meets with local notables in Nawa District. (U.S. Marine Corps photo)

The Lashkar Gah police remained after the election, and their continued presence was a source of considerable irritation to the district police chief, who saw them as a challenge to his authority. "He wanted them gone," recollected the sergeant, "and we told him he would have to take it up with the provincial chief of police."

Conclusion

The sergeant's tour as a PMT leader in Nawa District highlights some of the enduring challenges of police mentoring in Afghanistan. The district chief of police, who was more interested in maintaining his own position than in providing effective leadership for the men under his command, proved to be an insurmountable obstacle for his American advisor. Although mentors could attempt to influence the Afghans, they had no authority to remove ineffective or corrupt policemen.

By some measures, the U.S. Marine mentors made progress with the ANP's rank and file. During the run-up to FDD training, drug tests led to a decline in opiate use. Almost all of the district's police passed the course at the RTC in Kandahar. The police returned to Nawa with new uniforms, new equipment, and a new sense of pride, and ANP corruption appeared to drop.

Still, other indicators were less positive. Although they developed a new esprit de corps, the Nawa police showed no improvement in their tactical skills. In the sergeant's view, reduced police corruption was the result of the presence of vigilant Marines rather than a fundamental change in police morality.

The PMT adopted an approach that stressed mentoring by example. Professionalism and discipline on the part of the Marine mentors was intended to shape the behavior and outlook of the Nawa police. In the sergeant's opinion, the Marines did have a positive, "stiffening" effect on the ANP. How long this effect would persist, however, remained uncertain.

U.S. Marine Corps Police Mentor
Now Zad District, 2009

A gunnery sergeant serving with a military police (MP) company, 2d Marine Division, arrived in Now Zad District, Helmand Province, in August 2009.[79] As a member of a PMT,
he trained members of the district's Afghan National Police (ANP).

"Welfare Cases"

Some of the Afghan police had been trained by British mentors. They had uniforms,
and 10 of them had been through the Focused District Development, which vetted, re-
trained, reequipped, and mentored district police forces. But the 36 men that the sergeant was to mentor required substantial additional training.

"We had only a handful of guys who wanted to be legitimate police," he recalled. Conditions for ANP officers were poor. There were a lot of "welfare cases," he said. "They
weren't getting their basic needs met—food, warm clothing, vehicles." The district chief
of police did nothing to try to meet these shortfalls. Driven out by the Taliban in 2007,
the chief was "more concerned about his Land Rovers and getting a gift" now that he
was back, the Marine recalled.

Things Start to Get Hot

The team set up a training schedule for the ANP. For two weeks, the focus was on developing law enforcement skills, including checkpoint operations and vehicle and personnel searches. But then "things started to get hot again" when Taliban snipers began
operating in Now Zad, remembered the Marine advisor.

In addition to mentoring, the PMT had to serve as a quick-reaction force (QRF). "We
were called into action to assist the infantry who were pinned down by the enemy sniper

---

[79] Quotations used in this vignette are drawn from the author's interviews, Camp Lejeune, NC, 17
February 2010, and subsequent e-mail communications.

U.S. Marines in Now Zad District in April 2009.
(U.S. Marine Corps photo)

teams," he explained. "I had military working dogs that I used to track the enemy snipers to their positions and take them out." The team also provided security during the evacuation of civilian casualties and during joint Afghan National Army–Marine patrols. Continuing threats posed by the Taliban illustrated for the police mentor the importance of previous combat experience. "You needed to go to survival mode quickly," he said.

Police-Oriented Training

During the fall, security had improved to the point where the team could devote more attention to police-oriented training. "We tried to go beyond just having them go out and arrest people," the Marine advisor said. "The focus went from being aggressive to starting to collect names and intelligence on local bad guys." The PMT also attempted to foster relationships between the district police and village elders—a version of Western-style community policing in which law enforcement personnel worked with local residents to solve problems. "We had the ANP attend shuras and play mediator in things like land disputes," the Marine mentor recalled.

But overall, progress was slow. As in many other districts across Afghanistan, most of the ANP in Now Zad were illiterate, and a number of policemen were as young as 14 years old. A lack of formal education meant that Now Zad policemen generally lacked the discipline and persistence to absorb the PMT's mentoring. "They had a 10- to 15-minute attention span," the sergeant said. "We had to keep things very visual and do a lot of hands-on training."

The ANP's personnel system presented the mentors with other difficulties. Provincial police headquarters in Lashkar Gah was supposed to generate an ANP roster for the district but never did. As a result, it was impossible for the team to determine who was officially a policeman and who had been vetted by the Afghan authorities. Provincial headquarters also failed to provide a police recruiter, but according to the sergeant, no recruiter was willing to venture into the district.

Motivating the Now Zad police proved to be a considerable challenge. "They didn't want to run point on patrol," he recollected. "We had to use psychology on them." For exam-

U.S. Marines and an Afghan National Police officer on patrol in the Now Zad bazaar.
(U.S. Marine Corps photo)

ple, the PMT appealed to the Afghans' self-image as a culture of warriors: "I'd say to them, 'We hear back in the States that you're fierce warriors, but I'm not seeing it.'" The PMT pressed the police to take responsibility for planning and conducting their own operations, but with limited success. "We didn't go outside the wire without the ANP," the Marine said. "We pushed them to plan cordon-and-knock operations and raids. We'd tell them, 'You have information, this is your country, you're the police. What are you going to do about it?'"

A Question of Trust

In the sergeant's view, two other factors limited the ability of the mentors to make progress with the ANP. The first was the inability of the Marines to "get past" the differences they had with the Afghans. The problem was particularly acute with respect to rampant police corruption and criminality, which the ANP considered a normal part of being a police officer. The PMT found it hard to develop a sense of respect for men who engaged in illicit behavior to the degree the Now Zad ANP did.

The second factor was a lack of trust. Team members often found themselves second-guessing the Afghans and their motivations. In the case of the ANP's mediation of land disputes, for example, the police seemed to be acting in a positive way, but the Marine advisor often found himself wondering what the real agenda was behind their actions. "With the Afghans, who knows?" he wondered. He was also concerned about the ANP's loyalty. "How much do you really want to train them?" he asked. "After all, they can switch sides and join the Taliban."

Conclusion

The sergeant's experience in Now Zad highlights some of the major challenges that police mentors faced in many parts of Afghanistan. The security situation in Now Zad required the team to function as a QRF in addition to performing their mentoring duties. In his view, previous combat experience was invaluable in a mentoring environment that could quickly "get hot."

The police force was riddled with corruption, incompetence, and criminality. At the senior level, the district chief of police was unwilling or unable to improve the conditions of the men serving under his command. At the rank-and-file level, illiteracy and a lack of discipline made mentoring difficult.

Motivating the district police posed another serious challenge. The team prodded them to take responsibility for planning and conducting their operations and appealed to their sense of themselves as Afghan "warriors" to carry out their missions, but with limited effect.

Finally, the sergeant's tour with the Now Zad PMT exemplifies the importance of trust in effective police mentoring. The mentoring team found it impossible to look beyond the corruption and criminality that plagued the force. Widespread illicit behavior on the part of the police led the Marines to call into question the motivation of the men they were mentoring. The team also questioned the loyalty of the Now Zad police. Under such circumstances, it was impossible to create the bonds of trust and respect necessary for effective mentoring.

Conclusion

As illustrated in the preceding vignettes, the capabilities, performance, and leadership of the Afghan National Police (ANP)—like other Afghan institutions—differed from district to district, province to province, and region to region. In the view of a British police advisor in Lashkar Gah, the ANP showed signs of a growing commitment to serving and protecting the public. Specialized police units such as the Afghan National Civil Order Police (recruited on a national basis and provided with intensive and sustained advice, training, and support) displayed considerable professionalism and prowess. In many districts, however, the local police remained hobbled by drug addiction, endemic corruption, and poor leadership.

Senior Afghan police commanders also varied widely in terms of their commitment to protecting local communities and in their ability and motivation to provide effective leadership to the men under their command. In Helmand, for example, the provincial chief of police demonstrated to his UK mentor impressive leadership skills and a commitment to police reform. In Kunduz Province, however, the provincial police chief, who had spent $400,000 to acquire his post, used his position to prey on lucrative cross-border commercial traffic.

The experiences of American and British mentors also differed considerably. To some degree this was a function of the different backgrounds, perspectives, and attitudes U.S. and UK personnel brought to their missions. The availability of resources, the local conditions, and the caliber of the Afghans who received training and advice also played a part in shaping advisors' perceptions about the relative effectiveness of police mentoring.

Some mentors, such as the U.S. Marine police mentoring team (PMT) commander who served in Nawa-I-Barakzayi District, concluded that the presence of the Marines had a positive, "stiffening" effect on the Afghan police. However, police mentors in other districts had distinctly different experiences. A Marine PMT commander in Now Zad experienced intense frustration with ANP corruption and incompetence and found it impossible to forge effective working relationships with the Afghans.

2014 and Beyond

The themes highlighted in this study are likely to resonate in the years ahead as Afghans take on greater responsibility for their own security. This transition process is expected to unfold district by district and expand gradually across the country, with the army and police of the government of the Islamic Republic of Afghanistan assuming the lead role for security by the end of 2014. But this will not mean the end of the alliance's involvement in Afghan security. A "long-term partnership between NATO and Afghanistan . . . will endure beyond our combat mission," according to NATO Secretary General Anders Fogh Rasmussen.[80] This will almost certainly include advising, training, and equipping the ANP and other Afghan security forces.

Many of the challenges identified in this study are likely to persist during the transition period. NATO Training Mission–Afghanistan continues to face significant shortages of police mentors and trainers. The ANP is expanding, but the quality of the force—and in particular, its leadership—remains less than satisfactory, according to the U.S. Department of Defense (DOD).[81] And while the Afghan population as a whole expresses considerable confidence in the police, public support for the ANP in contested provinces like Helmand continues to drop.[82]

---

[80] "NATO and Afghanistan Launch Transition and Embark on a Long-Term Partnership," NATO, 20 November 2010, http://www.nato.int/cps/en/natolive/news_68728.htm, accessed 15 December 2010.

[81] DOD, *Report on Progress Toward Security and Stability in Afghanistan* (Washington: DOD, November 2010), 9

[82] According to a nationwide survey conducted jointly by the United Nations and the Afghan government, "73 percent of the Afghans polled said they have respect for the police and 71 percent confidence in its abilities." However, the same survey revealed that "in regions where police presence has been replaced by military operations, particularly in the southern areas such as Helmand, Afghans' confidence has fallen to 48 percent—down 19 points from a year ago." United Nations Advisory Mission in Afghanistan, "Majority of Afghans Positive About Local Police, Survey Shows," 3 February 2011, http://unama.unmissions.org/Default.aspx?tabid=1741&ctl=Details&mid=1882&ItemID=12228, accessed 2 March 2011.

Afghan National Police and village guard at
a checkpoint in Garmsir District, 2011.
(Photo courtesy of Patricio Asfura-Heim, CNA)

What this suggests is that mentors must be prepared for the kinds of conditions and operating environments discussed in this report. Although the ANP may make significant gains during the "Afghanization" of counterinsurgency and stability operations, it seems likely that inadequate leadership, illiteracy, and ill discipline will remain attributes of the police. Learning to manage our expectations for what the Afghans can reasonably achieve should be a key component of our approach to the ANP—both as the transition unfolds and after 2014.

Finally, the lessons identified in this study have utility beyond Afghanistan. Afghanistan (and Iraq) may have what one scholar terms a "strong inoculative effect on future interventions,"[83] and according to U.S. Defense Secretary Robert M. Gates, "[t]he odds of repeating another Afghanistan or Iraq—invading, pacifying, and administering a large third-world country—may be low."[84] Acting early to prevent what Gates terms "festering problems" from spinning out of control will obviate the need for large-scale military intervention later, in his view.[85] Building the capacity of local police—and, in some circumstances, the capacity of irregular, tribal, and informal policing structures—has an obvious role to play in a preventative approach to violent subnational conflict.

---

[83] James Gibney, "Masters of Peace," *Wilson Quarterly*, Winter 2011, 98.

[84] Thom Shanker, "Warning Against Wars Like Iraq and Afghanistan," *New York Times*, 25 February 2011, http://www.nytimes.com/2011/02/26/world/26gates.html, accessed 26 February 2011.

[85] Ibid.

Ideally, U.S. civilian agencies rather than the U.S. military should organize, train, equip, and advise law-enforcement institutions abroad. Since the mid-1970s, however, civilian departments have lacked both the capacity and, in many cases, the legal authority to assist foreign police forces. There are exceptions. The Departments of State, Treasury, and Justice perform specialized law enforcement training overseas, typically through contract personnel. But during and after violent conflicts over the past two decades, in countries ranging from Panama to Iraq to Afghanistan, U.S. armed forces (operating under legislative waivers) have been largely responsible for rebuilding local police institutions.

Given the potential demand for local police as an instrument to preempt conflict and the lack of standing international police assistance capabilities within U.S. civilian agencies—a condition that appears unlikely to change anytime soon—it seems probable that the American military will again be called upon to support foreign police institutions.[86] As in Afghanistan, those responsible for mentoring the police in other conflict zones will almost certainly encounter austere operating environments, official corruption and other malfeasance, and a shortage of human capital. In countries throughout the developing world, the police are typically impoverished and neglected relative to the armed forces. Advisors must be alert to the institutional, political, and even social constraints and limitations faced by the police they are called upon to mentor.

Police mentors must also recognize the inherent and fundamental contradiction between paramilitary forms of policing (with its heavy emphasis on weapons proficiency, vehicle checkpoints, and what one analyst terms other "higher end stability policing tasks such as riot control")[87] and what has been called "community," "democratic," or "core" policing. Ultimately, of course, resolving this contradiction—that is, deciding whether the police should be developed as a "force" or as a "service"—is the responsibility of policymakers rather than police mentors on the ground.

---

[86] For more on the lack of civilian police assistance capacity in the U.S. government, see Walter C. Ladwig III, "Training Foreign Police: A Missing Aspect of U.S. Security Assistance to Counterinsurgency," *Comparative Strategy* 26 (2007), 285–86.

[87] Dennis E. Keller, *U.S. Military Forces and Police Assistance in Stability Operations: The Least-Worst Option*, PKSOI Paper (Carlisle, PA: U.S. Army War College Strategic Studies Institute, August 2010), xiii.